THE RISE OF A
NEW WORLD ECONOMIC
POWER: POSTWAR TAIWAN

Recent Titles in
Contributions in Economics and Economic History

THE RISE OF A NEW WORLD ECONOMIC POWER: POSTWAR TAIWAN

Y. DOLLY HWANG

CONTRIBUTIONS IN ECONOMICS AND
ECONOMIC HISTORY,
NUMBER 121

Greenwood Press
New York • Westport, Connecticut • London

HC
430.5
H93
1991

Library of Congress Cataloging-in-Publication Data

Hwang, Y. Dolly.
  The rise of a new world economic power : postwar Taiwan / Y. Dolly
Hwang.
      p. cm.—(Contributions in economics and economic history,
  ISSN 0084–9235 ; no. 121)
  Includes bibliographical references and index.
  ISBN 0–313–26518–6 (alk. paper)
  1. Taiwan—Economic policy—1945–   2. Taiwan—Economic
conditions—1945–   3. Entrepreneurship—Taiwan.   I. Title.
II. Series.
  HC430.5.H93   1991
  338.95124'9—dc20   90–25219

British Library Cataloguing in Publication Data is available.

Library of Congress Catalog Card Number: 90–25219
ISBN: 0–313–26518–6
ISSN: 0084–9235

First published in 1991

Greenwood Press, 88 Post Road West, Westport, CT 06881
An imprint of Greenwood Publishing Group, Inc.

Printed in the United States of America

∞™

The paper used in this book complies with the
Permanent Paper Standard issued by the National
Information Standards Organization (Z39.48–1984).

10 9 8 7 6 5 4 3 2 1

To my parents
Captain and Mrs. Chiehshien Hwang
and my children
Vivian and Vallerie

CONTENTS

PREFACE

From the perspective of world history and global economics, the emergence of the newly industrialized countries (NICs) after World War II stands as one of the most significant events of the postwar era. While its impact on world politics and economic order has only begun to gain the attention of politicians and scholars and has increasingly become a subject of study and speculation, certainly the greatest value of the developing nations' economic success seems to have been the vast improvement in human life it has brought to these countries. This success would otherwise have been extremely difficult, if not impossible, to obtain. Taiwan's ability to transform itself from a poor country burdened with the usual Third World problems—stifling traditions, a large population, heavy foreign debts, and rampant inflation—into an emerging world economic power in a short period of forty-one years shines as a wondrous success story. It challenges the long-held pessimism of the insurmountability of world poverty problems and the human sufferings such problems spawn, and holds out genuine hope for achieving equality in the world economy and therefore perhaps a new vision of lasting world peace.

Just as a number of intertwining social, cultural, and institutional factors might have given rise to and perpetuated a vicious cycle of poverty and backwardness in China which locked the country into a state of underdevelopment for centuries, while the Western European nations and the United States had, one by one, made entrance to modern economic growth following the Industrial Revolution, so, too, the interplay of another set of social, cultural, and institutional factors in modern China might be responsible for breaking the vicious cycle on an island of China—Taiwan—and setting the island on a fast road to modern economic growth. The major task of this book is to identify these factors and trace their intricate and dynamic operations in a course that spans two centuries beginning with China's struggle for modernization and extending to Taiwan's recent economic success.

The focal points of investigation in presenting the interrelations between these factors and Taiwan's economic growth are as follows. A series of political, social, cultural, and institutional revolutions in China began shortly after the Opium War of 1845, which historians mark as the beginning of modern Chinese history. These violent changes did not conclude until 1949 when the Nationalist government relocated on the island of Taiwan, and began to modernize the island's economy. For China to break the thousands of years of stagnation which resulted from its rigid traditions and customs and to introduce the changes necessary to promote modern economic growth, a superpowerful force was required. Such a force was Chinese nationalism which developed in the latter part of the nineteenth century amidst a wave of foreign aggressions. Even today the nationalist spirit plays a significant role in Taiwan, uniting its government and people in their striving for more economic miracles. Traditionally, the Chinese government had been closely involved in major areas of Chinese life. It was therefore natural that the Nationalist government would assume a dominant role in Taiwan's economic development. Its iron resolve and skillful leadership have been prime factors in Taiwan's economic success.

Most of Taiwan's economic policies are aimed at directing the operation of economic forces to effect planned changes beneficial to economic development; therefore, a study of the country's economic policies will provide a close look at its development strategies. The success of Taiwan's economy has hinged on the performance of its manufacturing exports. Accordingly, by tracing the development of its industry and international trade and analyzing its development strategies, we will obtain considerable insights into Taiwan's economic success.

The evolution of Taiwan's fiscal policies and financial institutions reveals the adaptations its government has made to facilitate economic growth. Confucianism, once regarded as antithetical to capitalism, appears to have bred a unique brand of capitalism in the Far East which has helped provide the highly energetic capitalist spirit that characterizes Taiwan business and industry. The highly aggressive entrepreneurial drive of Taiwanese businesspeople has led to the establishment of an unusually large number of able small- and medium-sized enterprises. Their high operating efficiency and their customer-accommodating flexibility have drawn manufacturing export orders to the island and have enabled the economy to adjust quickly to the turbulent changes of international markets. Thus, exports have become the backbone of Taiwan's economy. As is true of all newly industrialized countries, access to international capital, technologies, and markets has been crucial to Taiwan's economic success. Therefore, any examination of this success would not be complete without a discussion of international inputs to the success.

How did Taiwan attain its status as a world-class economic power? Both in the culture as a whole and within the individual Chinese people there has always been a strong impulse to seek after the highest possible welfare for themselves, their families, and their fellow countrymen. When values and institutions in Chinese society which had obstructed economic growth were removed, and favorable ones installed, this powerful force was allowed to operate at its fullest power, placing Taiwan on the road to remarkable economic advancement. Therefore, judgments made about China's poor development prospects as recently as sixty years ago were erroneous, for they failed to recognize the mighty latent force that lay beneath China's seemingly helpless situation.

Taiwan's economic progress in the last forty-one years has been accompanied by rapid, large-scale improvements in the island's political, social, educational, and health and welfare spheres, which would otherwise be difficult to achieve. Advancements achieved in these areas in turn made possible Taiwan's further economic growth. As the rapid growth of the economy continues, it is being gradually assimilated into the integral body of the world economy. Thus, Taiwan has contributed to the stability and growth of the world economy. Once Taiwan embarked on a course of modern growth, it exhibited a remarkable ability to narrow the technological gap between itself and the industrial nations. This ability makes the economy a power to reckon with. In addition, Taiwan's demand for materials, parts, and inexpensive labor has contributed to the economic development of a number of South Asian countries.

The emphasis of this book is on the dynamic changes that have taken place in Chinese society in the last one hundred and fifty years and on the interplay between cultural and institutional adjustments and economic growth. We discuss how major events in modern Chinese history contributed to the inevitability of Taiwan's rise to economic power. Our discussion encompasses the Opium War and the ensuing unequal treaties between China and foreign powers which awakened the complacent, tradition-bound Chinese to the urgent need to modernize; the victory of the Chinese revolution which led to the founding of the Chinese republic; the challenges and reforms during the republic's mainland period; the surrender of the Japanese at the end of World War II and the subsequent retrocession of Taiwan to China; the defeat of the Nationalists at the hands of the Chinese Communists and the following retreat of the Nationalist government to the island; the break out of the Korean War and the resumption of U.S. economic aid to Taiwan; and the fight for survival under Communist threats and the self-help of the Nationalist government. In addition, we consider the prospect of closer economic cooperation between Taiwan and mainland China and the renunification of the two Chinas in the near future. All such speculations on future Asian history should be of great interest to the history-minded reader.

Students of economics, on the other hand, will find the account of Taiwan's rising economy a good case study for testing the cross-cultural applicability of economic theories, most of which were founded on studies of Western industrial nations. This book's examination of the developmental experience of Taiwan's economy might be helpful to the effort to build an integrated economic development theory of the Third World. Those who see as significant the emergence of the Far East's four new industrialized economies—Hong Kong, Korea, Singapore, and Taiwan—might find this book's in-depth analysis of Taiwan's economy useful in projecting changes which these economies might effect in the world economy. Those readers interested in international trade might find our investigation of the interplay of foreign capital, technology, equipment, materials, and markets and Taiwan's development of export industries useful in assessing the potentials of, and predicting trends in, Taiwan's imports and exports.

Finally, those readers interested in international politics should find our discussion of the role of the United States and Japan in the development of Taiwan's economy, as well as Taiwan's role in stimulating the economic development of some of the Southeast Asian countries, helpful in understanding the economic forces that shape international politics. In our analyses, only minimum use is made of technical jargon and we assume a background uncluttered by too many economic theories. Readers who have a general interest in world affairs will find the contents of this book very accessible.

Acknowledgments are due to the following institutions for making research materials available: Jackson Library at the University of North Carolina at Greensboro, the China Institute of Economics at Taipei, the Academia Sinica at Taipei, the China External Trade Development Council, the Council for Economic Planning and Development of Executive Yuan of the Republic of China, and the Ministry of Economic Affairs of the Republic of China. I owe special thanks to Minister Kwoh-Ting Li for reading the manuscript and giving valuable advice. The assistance provided by Tony Lee of the New York office of the China External Trade Development Council was important to my research. I am grateful to the following individuals for providing information and special insights: Wen-Pau Chang, Bing-Queng Chiang, Tseng-Ti Chiang, Dr. K. Casey Chuang, Stephen K. Craven, Dr. H. Steve Hsieh, K. Y. Lee, Dr. Yung-San Lee, T. H. Lin, Richard R. C. Liu, Yen-Shing Pan, Dr. C. T. Shih, Stanley Shih, Philip C. M. Wang, C. M. Wang, Professor Tso-Yuong Wang, K. H. Wu, Dr. Shih-Chien Yang, and Wan-An Yeh.

THE RISE OF A
NEW WORLD ECONOMIC
POWER: POSTWAR TAIWAN

1 INTRODUCTION

Following the Chinese Nationalist government's relocation to Taiwan in 1949, economic development on the island for the next forty-one years produced an impressive record of achievement. Despite the disruptive effects of the oil crises in the 1970s, economic growth on Taiwan has maintained an average annual rate of 8.7 percent, compared with an annual average growth rate of 3.8 percent for industrial nations and 4.8 percent for developing nations.[1] In terms of the trade volume on the international market, Taiwan, with land area about the size of Rhode Island and with limited natural resources, progressed from sixtieth among the world's nations in 1949 to thirteenth in 1989. In fact, Taiwan's trade volume with the United States in 1988 made Taiwan the United States' fourth largest trading partner for that year followed by Canada, Japan, and West Germany.[2] Taiwan has also made commendable progress in per capita income; it rose from U.S. $50 in 1949 to U.S. $7,500 in 1989. When examining these and other statistics of Taiwan's economic development taken in the last forty years against those of Japan recorded during the years of its economic development, economists have noted that what took Japan fifty years to accomplish was reached by the Taiwanese in just half that time.[3] This kind of performance has prompted some observers to call Taiwan's achievement an economic miracle.

Today, Taiwan ventures out to the world experimenting with different possibilities to expand its role in world economic affairs. Its development loans to mainland China, Thailand, Malaysia, the Philippines, and some South American countries have become increasingly important to the economic development of these countries. Taiwan's new trade policy permits, for the first time in forty-one years, direct trade with Eastern European countries and with Russia. This complete reversal of the government's position since 1949 on contacts with Communist countries has opened up a whole new horizon of export markets for Taiwanese products. Not surprisingly, the ingenuity and diligence of Taiwan's industry in product development and improvement have started to pay off; a growing number of Taiwanese manufacturing products now command sizable shares of the world market. Taiwan has been effectively using its growing economic power to regain diplomatic recognition in the world community. The Taiwanese government lost that recognition in 1972 after the United States reestablished its diplomatic ties with the Chinese Communist regime.

Taiwan's astonishing economic performance has not come from, as is the case with some of the oil-rich countries, a sudden rocketing appreciation of its natural resources; its economy has maintained a steady high rate of growth in the last twenty-five years. If Taiwan continues its current efforts to modernize its labor law, financial institutions, industrial waste management and pollution control, welfare services, and political structure, the economy's high growth rate will certainly be carried into its next developmental stages.

Our study of postwar Taiwan's economic growth will go beyond just giving a sensational account of the economic achievements of one of the four phenomenal Far East "economic dragons," nor will we merely offer a comparative analysis of the Eastern and Western economies as has usually been the case. In this way, we may provide answers to a number of often asked questions concerning the origin and process of economic development in Taiwan in particular and in the Third World nations in general. Taiwan's rags-to-riches experience naturally inspires a number of general questions concerning how the Taiwanese accomplished such remarkable success in a relatively short period of time and under obvious adverse circumstances. Given that cultural factors might have played a role in this success, the country's experience can be of great value to other developing nations. Then, we might ask, what lessons can be learned from Taiwan's experience?

During the last forty-one years, swift and drastic changes have facilitated the island's economic growth. In light of these changes, how do some of the economic development theories, especially those identifying changes accompanying economic development, stand against Taiwan's developmental experience? How can a developing nation accomplish the difficult transition from an agricultural to an industrial economy? How can a developing nation achieve rapid economic growth without paying the heavy price of polarizing wealth in its society—creating the dichotomy between urban and rural residents, between the agricultural and industrial sectors, and between business owners and laborers? Moreover, how can a developing nation that receives capital and technological assistance from industrial nations avoid dependency on the economy of these nations, as some economists so bleakly predicted?[4] How can a developing nation overcome the deeply entrenched problem of government corruption, which commonly plagued Third World nations, and proceed to economic success? What is the government's role in the economic success of a developing nation?

The economic success of Taiwan and other Far Eastern countries has been commonly viewed as examples of non-Western nations that have followed in Japan's footsteps, making gigantic strides into the modern economy, which had previously been attainable only by Western countries. Since Japan, Taiwan, and other Far East NICs—Hong Kong, Singapore, and Korea—all share a strong Confucian tradition, we may naturally speculate that Confucian philosophy created a unique subculture of capitalism that was responsible for the emergence of the modern economies and later, for the astonishing economic achievements of these countries. If this is true, then, what is this Asian subculture of capitalism, and how did it move the economy in Taiwan to its success?

Entrepreneurship is an important ingredient of Western economies. What is the role of entrepreneurship in the emergence of a modern economy in Taiwan? How did government policy there encourage the exercise of entrepreneurial spirit to build the island's economy? What are the strengths and weaknesses of this structure in terms of the future growth of the economy?

Granted that economic policies, institutions, and social structures in a growing economy are constantly evolving to adjust to the new challenges produced by economic growth, what evolutionary process is taking place in governmental policies, financial institutions, and economic structure in Taiwan?

For fifteen years, from 1950 to 1965, the United States pumped a large sum of economic aid into Taiwan, and since 1949, the United States has been Taiwan's foremost trade partner. On the other hand, Taiwan has a history of Japanese colonization (from 1895 to 1945), and the island's geographical proximity to Japan has made that country the primary source of Taiwan's imports. Furthermore, the United States and Japan continue to be the main foreign investors in Taiwan. The existence of these and other business relationships between Taiwan and the United States and Japan prompts questions about the role of these two powers in Taiwan's economic growth.

Economic success has prompted Taiwan to extend itself in the international community. What will become of this island country when it increases its involvement in the international community, especially with those Asian countries with whom it has built close business ties, and with some South American and African developing countries to whom it has given sizable economic assistance?

Finally, does nationalism play any role in the economic modernization of developing countries? What is its role in Taiwan's economic development success? Many China observers view Taiwan's success as the long overdue fruit of China's modernization efforts which began approximately a century ago; nationalism, as is the case with many other Third World nations, played a strong role in producing the modernization efforts in China. This book will address each of these questions.

Both historians and economists view the postwar emergence of modern economies as one of the major developments of the twentieth century. This development is perhaps epitomized by achieving the status of newly industrialized country (NIC) by Hong Kong, Korea, Taiwan, and Singapore. Simon Kuznets, a Nobel laureate in economics, has compared the experiences of all the economies that have entered into the modern epoch of growth, including those industrially advanced nations that made their transition one or two centuries ago and those that did so during this century. Kuznets concludes that certain factors present in these economies have allowed them to make such a transition. Among the factors he lists are population growth, increase in productivity, acquisition of modern technologies, and elimination of institutional obstacles.[5] Circumstances and mechanisms that contributed to the presence of these factors in NICs are presumably different from those responsible for their presence in eighteenth-century England or early nineteenth-century Western Europe and America. For example, government policies and planning, strategic technology transfers, international corporations, and foreign capital are all instrumental to the increase of productivity and the acquisition of technologies in all NIC economies. This was not true of industrially advanced economies a century or two ago. These and other general characteristics give extra meaning to the study of the transitional experience of Taiwan, for they offer a view of some of the commonly shared experiences of all NICs.

Theories that might explain how Taiwan, a Third World nation, achieved such extraordinary economic success would be of particular interest to developing countries. Recently, for the first time, the People's Republic of China acknowledged the economic success of Taiwan, its bitter foe for the last forty years, and appealed to its people to learn from Taiwan's experience. Both the Export Processing Zones that were built in the last few years at the southern seaports of China, and the Communist government's development strategy that guided the establishment of these zones—to spur the development of mainland China's economy—appear to be exact duplications of what occurred in Taiwan some thirty years ago. In Taiwan itself, both the government and the people have been enthusiastic about sharing their successful experience with the mainland Chinese, in an attempt to help them to build their economy.

Taiwan's economic success has also been a source of inspiration to Southeast Asian countries. The United States' gradual reduction of its import quotas for Taiwanese products in the last few years, motivated primarily to balance its foreign trade with the island, forced Taiwanese manufacturers to relocate their plants to Southeast Asian countries, such as Thailand, Malaysia, and the Philippines, so that they could take advantage of the unused U.S. import quotas there. Furthermore, the sharp acceleration of the value of the Taiwanese currency—40 percent in the last four years, as against the U.S. dollar—greatly reduced the competitiveness of the Taiwanese labor cost in the international market. As a result, the low labor cost in these Southeast Asian countries became attractive to the Taiwanese manufacturers who had contemplated plant relocation. Naturally, the desire of these countries to emulate Taiwan's economic success was enhanced by their increasingly close business relations with the Taiwanese. As has been observed, the number of government-level economic conferences between Taiwan and these Southeast countries has risen lately, as has the number of joint business ventures. Because of Taiwans cultural affinity and geographical proximity with these countries, and the presence of a high percentage of Chinese immigrants in these countries' business communities, Taiwan can serve as an economic development model for these countries.

Taiwan has also gained admirers in Africa. In the summer of 1989, Nigeria hosted a world trade conference and chose Taiwan's economic development experience as the conference theme. Tunisia, in the fall of 1989, sent an invitation to Taiwan to establish an official trade office in that country. The government in Tunisia hoped that the trade office would facilitate the flow of Taiwanese investment and technology into the country, especially in the area of textiles, electronics, and shipbuilding, to help ameliorate the country's unemployment problem. Having provided agricultural technological assistance to a number of African countries in the 1960s, Taiwan welcomes any opportunity to resume its economic assistance activities in Africa.

Forty-one years of careful economic planning and hard drive have produced enormous prosperity in Taiwan. As a result of their newly acquired wealth, new possibilities have become available to this nation, specifically the pursuit of further economic growth, the modernization of its political structure and process, and the restoration of its national prestige within the international community. At the same time, their economic success has presented the Taiwanese with grave new challenges:

- Growing protectionism in the United States and Western Europe, the very two markets on which the performance of Taiwan's exports has come to depend.

- The sudden sharp rise of the currency value of the Taiwanese dollar as against the U.S. dollar following a quarter century of stable foreign exchange rates between these two currencies.

- The subsequent loss of international comparative advantages in labor cost which have placed the future of Taiwan's economy at a crossroad.

An analysis of the strengths of the economy which were responsible for its success should be of value to the Taiwanese people as they try to chart a course for the future.

In the late 1970s, Taiwan became a subject of study by development economists. The first group of economists went to Taiwan as foreign consultants to the government and later published their analyses and assessments; these were the earliest works on the subject done by outside scholars.[6] Economic statistics compiled by the Taiwanese government since the early 1950s have been the major source of data for research workers on the subject. Government-sponsored publications in Taiwan tend to focus on the evolution of economic policies and the quantitative documentation of the conditions that warrant the policies. Perhaps because of the lack of alternative sources, these publications became frequently referenced materials. For example, the widely quoted theory on the three developmental stages of Taiwan's economy was built on the statistics and information provided in these publications.

Local Taiwanese economists have had a strong interest in establishing links between the achievements of the economy and the government's economic planning and policy. Their research efforts have helped document Taiwan's economic achievements and the government policies responsible.[7] In recent years, they have adopted a new research interest: they support the call for removing the government presence in Taiwan's economy to make room for a free market economy. On the other hand, international economists tend to explain Taiwan's modern economic growth based on a structural analysis; this tendency is attributable to the theoretical interests of those economists such as Simon Kuznets, who provide consultations to the Taiwanese government.

Kuznets' economic development theory attempts to explain the emergence of the postwar modern economic growth in Third World countries as well as eighteenth- and nineteenth-century economic advances in what are today's developed nations. According to his theory, during the second half of the eighteenth century the Industrial Revolution in England was one of a series of epochs in world economic history which was marked by a consistent application of available scientific knowledge, both technological and social, to the continuing advancement of production tools and methods. This modern mode of economic growth spread to all of Western Europe and to its overseas offshoots, the United States and Canada. In the late nineteenth century, it spread to Japan and, in the 1930s, to Russia. In Kuznets' view, following World War II, the presence of a sustainable high growth rate in some South American and Asian economies was a direct result of this spread of modern economic growth. Some countries achieved modern economic growth at later points in time because of their respective historical heritages, political and economic institutions, and different degrees of readiness.

Kuznets' theory asserts that as the economy undergoes modern economic growth an unusually high rate of growth in population and per capita product becomes evident. Kuznets views a sharp rise in per capita product as being largely the result of a rise in efficiency, that is, in output per unit of input. Although a high rate of per capita product accompanied by an increasing rate of per unit efficiency has been identified as the fundamental characteristics of modern economic growth, he goes on to identify the second characteristic as being a high rate of structural shifts in society. Structural shifts, Kuznets states, are to be found in the shares of various industries in output, labor force, or the stock of material capital; in the composition of the labor force; in private and government sector shares; in the life patterns associated with per capita income and attachment to different industries; in the ratio between savings and consumption; in the factoral and size distribution of income; and in the composition and relative importance of exports and imports, and hence in the nature of international economic relations.[8] Kuznets observes that the application of science to problems of economic production and human welfare has actually led to modern economic growth.

Yet, the application of science to economic production via technology presupposes the presence of a proper social climate that fosters both the pursuit and application of science.[9] Such a climate can only be produced in developing countries, in Kuznets' view, by changing the social institutions that have been antithetic to the society's tendency to exploit the stock of technological knowledge accumulated through the economic growth experience of the developed countries. Kuznets predicts that as the growth of an economy takes off, a continuing dynamic interplay takes place between applications of technology and changes in social institution; applications of technology stimulate institutional changes, which in turn make possible the further application of technology. Kuznets' theory has heavily influenced the analytical framework used in this book to explain the rise of Taiwan's economy to world power status.

Kuznets uses a chain relation to explain a nation's entrance into modern economic growth: social and institutional changes make possible the application of scientific knowledge to production, and the application of scientific knowledge leads to modern economic growth. This chain relation seems to offer some direction for solving the puzzling questions concerning economic growth in Taiwan. For example, why did the Chinese, a people with a long early history of scientific and technological innovation, civilization, and bureaucracy not experience modern economic growth until the 1960s? Why did Taiwan's economy take off immediately following the Nationalist government's relocation to the island? And while the people on Taiwan share the same culture and history with the people on the mainland, why were the Taiwanese able to begin their modern growth in the early 1960s, yet only in the last few years, have signs of economic growth been visible on mainland China?

During the last 150 years, China has experienced changes unprecedented in its history. For the first time it opened its doors to foreign trade and Western influence. It was China's resistance to Western economic expansion that brought it into wars with the West. Its defeats in these wars subjected China to unequal treaties with Western countries. The Chinese indignation and shame over these unequal treaties triggered the outburst of their long-harbored discontent with the Chinese imperial government and its rule. Soon the discontent turned into harsh demand for political and social reform. At that time, the country's intellectuals proposed the total modernization of the country, with an emphasis on the wholesale transfer of Western technology into China, as a general reform direction. The modernization effort had precipitated the Chinese revolution of 1911 which ended thousands of years of rule by the Chinese Dynasty and gave birth to the Chinese republic. From that point on, China became involved in a long struggle to transform itself into a modern nation. This book examines the social and institutional changes that occurred in China during this transformation period, changes that were necessary to prepare the country to achieve modern economic growth.

In later chapters we describe Taiwan's rise to world economic status from different perspectives—the institutional and cultural transformation of Chinese society, the foreign inputs into Taiwan's economic growth, the role of the Nationalist government, Taiwan's foreign trade, industrialization, and economic policies, the role of small- and medium-sized businesses in the economy, and the development of Confucian capitalism in the Chinese culture. We will show that changes in Chinese society and in the life of the Chinese people in the last 150 years in effect removed structural obstacles and prepared Taiwan to become a modern nation. Chapter 2 examines Taiwan's economic development process of the last forty-one years and assesses its economic achievements. Chapter 3 presents a brief historical account of China's struggle to become a modernized nation and explains how this transformation prepared China for modern growth which was finally actualized in Taiwan in the 1960s. Chapter 4 looks at the motivational forces of Chinese nationalism in Taiwan's economic success. Chapter 5 discusses the culturally based obligation of the Chinese government to the economic well-being of the Chinese people, how the evolution of the Chinese government in modern times enabled the government to provide effective leadership in Taiwan's economic development, and the government's leadership in Taiwan's economic success. Chapter 6 studies the characteristics and evolution of Taiwan's economic policies. Chapter 7 begins to trace Taiwan's economic policies. Chapter 7 begins to trace Taiwan's industrialization process with the Japanese colonial development and moves on to the Nationalist government's postwar restoration effort, the import substitution period, the export expansion period, the promotion of the island's heavy and petrochemical industry, and finally to the present development of the high tech industry. Chapter 8 examines how the government's policy skillfully steered the development and growth of the island's foreign trade from an inward-oriented to an export-oriented growth and discusses Taiwan's counter strategy to the new surge of trade protectionism. Chapter 9 traces the evolution of Taiwan's monetary and fiscal policies and studies the modernization process of its financial institutions. Chapter 10 attempts to explain how modern challenges to Confucianism have given birth to a new brand of capitalism in Chinese culture and how this brand of capitalism has affected the business behavior of the Taiwanese. Chapter 11 discusses the cultural origin of the Chinese entrepreneurial spirit and the role of the entrepreneur in Taiwan's economy. The contributions made by small- and medium-sized businesses to Taiwan's economy are examined. Chapter 12 analyzes the influence of the United States and Japan on Taiwan's economic development. The impact of U.S. economic aid, as well as the extent to which Taiwan's economy has depended on trade with the United States and Japan, is also assessed. Chapter 13 identifies future trends with respect to Taiwan's export markets, the prospect of depoliticization, the development of industry, and the improved quality of life in the fast growing economy.

NOTES

1. Executive Yuan, Council on Economic Development, *The Journey of the Modernization of Taiwan's Economy* (Taipei: Bureau of Economic Research, 1987), p. 1.

2. Ibid., p. 53.

3. Kazushi Ohkawa and Gustav Ranis, eds., *Japan and the Developing Countries* (New York: Oxford University Press, 1985), p. 13.

4. Frederick C. Deyo, ed., *The Political Economy of the New Asian Industrialism* (Ithaca, N.Y.: Cornell University Press, 1987).

5. Simon Kuznets, *Modern Economic Growth—Rate, Structure, and Speed* (New Haven, Conn.: Yale University Press, 1966).

6. See Walter Galenson, *Economic Growth and Structural Change in Taiwan: The Postwar Experience of the Republic of China* (Ithaca, N.Y.: Cornell Universtiy Press, 1979); Jan S. Prybyla, *The Societal Objectives of Wealth, Stability, and Equality in Taiwan* (Baltimore: University of Maryland Press, 1978); John Fei, *Growth with Equality* (London: Oxford University Press, 1979).

7. See Kwoh-Ting Li, *The Evolution of Policy Behind Taiwan's Development Success* (New Haven, Conn.: Yale University Press, 1988); Mo-Huan Hsing, *Taiwan: Industrialization and Policies* (London: Oxford University Press, 1971), Ching-Yuan Lin, *Industrialization in Taiwan, 1946–1972* (New York: Praeger, 1973); Kwoh-Ting Li and Tzong-Shian Yu, *Experiences and Lessons of Economic Development in Taiwan* (Taipei: Academia Sinica, 1982); Tso-Yuong Wang, *Economic Miracle* (Taipei: Time Publishing, 1984).

8. Simon Kuznets, *Postwar Economic Growth* (Cambridge, Mass.: Harvard University Press, 1964), pp. 44–45.

9. Kuznets, *Modern Economic Growth*, pp. 12–13.

2 ECONOMIC DEVELOPMENT IN TAIWAN

Chinese historians and economists have noted that modern economic development in Taiwan actually started during the Japanese colonization period. This period began in 1895 when Taiwan was ceded to Japan as restitution for war damages following the Sino-Japanese War and ended in 1945 when the island was retroceded to China subsequent to the Japanese surrender at the close of World War II.[1] During the colonial period, under a policy of "agriculturalizing Taiwan and industrializing Japan," the Japanese invested heavily in the island's agriculture. In addition to capital investments in the agricultural processing plants, the Japanese brought in new crops, constructed irrigation systems, introduced the use of chemical fertilizers, and organized the farmers' credit union and the farmers' association. As a result, a typical colonial economic relationship was formed between Japan and Taiwan. During this period, most of Taiwan's agricultural products were exported to Japan in exchange for manufactured goods. By 1939 all the perceived developmental potential of Taiwan's agriculture, forestry, and fishery industries to the service of the Japanese Empire had been thoroughly exploited by the colonial administration. Taiwan's main agricultural products during this period were rice and sugar; their peak production under colonial rule was reached in 1939.[2]

Thereafter agricultural production declined sharply, until by the last years of World War II it had deteriorated badly. A number of factors were responsible for this deterioration. For one thing, Allied bombings had inflicted extensive damage on Taiwan. In addition, a series of floods had devastated a large portion of the farmland. Excessive Japanese wartime military expenses had left the island's infrastructure, including irrigation systems, unmaintained. The war had made it difficult for the Taiwanese to obtain a steady supply of chemical fertilizers from Japan. Moreover, the Taiwanese farms experienced a severe labor shortage after most of the young males were drafted into the Japanese military. During the war, the colonial government instituted a rice purchasing and rationing policy to ensure that a sufficient amount of rice would be shipped to Japan for military consumption. Naturally, the policy depressed the Taiwanese farmer's motivation to produce, bringing agricultural production down to its lowest point. In 1945, when Taiwan rejoined China, the island's total agricultural production barely amounted to 45 percent of its peak record set in 1939.[3]

Industrial growth in Taiwan during the prewar colonial period was slow. The primary industry during that time was sugar and tea processing, and food canning. Although there were some rudimentary cement and paper mills and chemical fertilizer plants, the production of these industries was insignificant. In 1937, in preparation for war, the Japanese Cabinet decided to launch a five-year economic development plan on Taiwan, the first economic plan ever designed for and implemented there. The industrial component of the plan was, of course, dedicated to Japanese military needs. In addition to expanding the existing industries, the plan called for establishing the textile, chemical, steel, oil refinery, shipbuilding, and metallurgy industries in Taiwan. In 1940 Taiwan's industrial production reached its highest prewar level. Later, Allied bombings damaged much of the island's industrial facilities. The wartime difficulties in obtaining industrial materials plus a serious labor shortage further crippled industrial production. When the war was over in 1945, industrial production was only about one-third that of its highest prewar record.

During the colonial period, the railroads and highways were extended to Taiwan's remote areas. However, during the war, air bombings and lack of maintenance rendered more than half of this system unusable. During the latter part of the war, plans were drawn up to build new ports on the island. Before the construction was even completed, the bombings destroyed all of what had been built.

During the colonial period, Japan automatically became Taiwan's number one trade partner. At one point, trade with Japan constituted more than 90 percent of Taiwan's total foreign trade. Rice and sugar represented the primary exports to Japan, and manufactured goods were the major import items from that country. The war impaired Taiwan's exports, and the wartime shipping difficulties caused severe shortages of supplies on the island. As a result, high inflation set in. During the last two years of the war, inflation reached an annual rate of 68 percent, and when the war ended, the rate had risen to 300 percent.[4]

Taiwan's economy was in profound shambles when the Nationalist government took over in 1945. To bring the runaway inflation under control, the government instituted a series of economic stabilization measures. Since the colonial Japanese had forbidden the Taiwanese from occupying any managerial positions, and with the Japanese now repatriated, Taiwan had no trained managerial personnel. Technical specialists and managers were soon flown in from the mainland to operate the business enterprises the Japanese had left behind. Unwittingly, this expedient action started what would become a high ratio of state enterprises in Taiwan's economy; in addition, a high proportion of the mainlanders held managerial positions in government. Some of these specialists and managers were assigned to operate state enterprises and others to reconstruct war-damaged plants and infrastructures so that production could quickly be resumed.

At that time, the government believed that only by normalizing material supplies would the island have a chance to control inflation. To restore Taiwan's agriculture, the government assisted in returning displaced farmers to their land, thereby ensuring an adequate supply of agricultural labor, repaired damaged irrigation systems, advocated various improvement measures of the farming technologies, and guaranteed a sufficient supply of chemical fertilizers. Soon, agriculture began to show signs of recovery. In 1949, only four years after the war, agricultural production regained 85 percent of its prewar peak capacity. Later, land reforms and the reorganization of the farmers' association made great contributions to enhancing the farmer's production incentives. In 1952 Taiwan's agriculture regained its highest prewar production capacity.

Taiwan's postwar industrial restoration efforts were aimed chiefly at rebuilding its industrial plants and resuming the infrastructure construction projects started under Japanese colonial rule. When the restoration tasks were barely completed, the Nationalist government immediately began to promote the development of new industries. At the time, however, financial and personnel constraints resulted from the war and the resettlement of the government forced it to carefully prioritize its industrial development plan. Only three industries were selected to be developed first: electrical power, textiles, and fertilizers. (Electrical power was the primary source of energy, and the island's imports of textile products and chemical fertilizers had been consuming a good chunk of its scarce foreign currency reserves.) Other industries that experienced expansion during this period were flour processing, cement, oil refinery, paper, chemical, and steel. The new industries built in this era included the sewing machine, bicycle, and electrical fan. In 1952 Taiwan's industrial production, as had its agricultural production, finally reached its prewar peak level.[5]

The railroads and highways were among the first to be repaired in the postwar restoration effort. By 1949 the seaports had been rebuilt to their prewar capacity. During the same year, various shipping enterprises with a combined shipping capacity of about 40,000 tons were successfully relocated to Taiwan from the mainland, which in time gave Taiwan its urgently needed sea transportation means.

During the war, Taiwan's foreign trade was totally disrupted, and it was able to resume only when a trade treaty with Japan was signed in 1949. U.S. economic aid to Taiwan, which started in the following year, provided the funds Taiwan needed to import equipment and materials for its export manufacturing industries. In 1952 Taiwan's total foreign trade volume was a meager U.S. $320 million, of which $120 million was for export and $200 million for import. Rice and sugar accounted for 78 percent of total exports, and more than half of the exported rice and sugar went to Japan. Among the items imported to Taiwan during the year, cotton and fertilizer constituted a quarter of total imports, and flour, soy beans, crude oil, metal, and medicine made up one-third of imports. More than half of Taiwan's imports in 1952 came from the United States and 30 percent from Japan.

In this same year Taiwan's agricultural and industrial production volume reached its highest prewar level, and the arrival of a large sum of agricultural products under the U.S. economic aid program significantly eased the country's supply shortage. As a result, inflation went down and prices became stabilized. At this time, the Taiwanese saw their opportunity to embark on an ambitious economic development endeavor. As an application requirement for U.S. economic aid, a comprehensive plan for developing the island's economy had been established. The plan consisted of the Nationalist government's strategy for resource allocations for its economic development effort. Starting in 1953, a series of six-year and two four-year economic plans were implemented.

Beginning in 1952, GNP started a steady rise at an 8.7 percent annual rate, which is much higher than the average rate of 3.8 percent achieved by the developed nations during the same period of time. Per capita income also rose from around U.S. $50 in 1949 to approximately U.S. $7,500 in 1989.[6] Taiwanese economists have identified four stages of economic growth in the 1945–89 period.

The first stage began in 1945 and was completed in 1952. This was a period of turmoil and instability on Taiwan. The Japanese surrender in

1945 was followed by the repatriation of the Japanese and the return of the island to the Nationalist Chinese. Four years later, the Nationalists lost the mainland to the Chinese Communists and sought retreat in Taiwan. With an annual inflation rate as high as 300 percent, the island had to find ways to accommodate millions of retreated government troops and refugees from the mainland. Therefore, during this period economic development focused on the quick repair of war-damaged infrastructures and the resumption of agricultural and industrial production in order to bring inflation under control and to stabilize the economy.

In the second stage, which ran from 1953 to 1960, two consecutive four-year economic development plans were implemented. In these years U.S. economic aid pumped, on the average, U.S. $1.5 billion a year into the economy.[7] This enormous economic aid gave the government of Taiwan a firm financial basis to fight inflation with skillfully maneuvered fiscal and monetary policies. Soon after the inflation rate was brought down to below 10 percent per year, the economy began to grow at an annual rate of 7.6 percent. Simultaneously, the population also experienced a high growth, 3.5 percent per year, which offset the economic growth to an unimpressive 4 percent annual GNP growth rate. In the meantime, the ambitious industrial development efforts generated a wave of import demands for industrial equipment and materials. In addition, the rapid population growth, which was also accompanied by a rising living standard, forced the resource-poor island to further expand its imports. Inevitably, Taiwan was driven into a deep trade imbalance. Troubled by the economy's growing dependence on foreign imports, the government adopted an import substitution policy to encourage new industries to produce goods to replace imports.

The third economic development stage spanned a period of twelve years, from 1961 to 1972. This stage was marked by rigorous economic growth and Taiwan's economic independence from foreign aid. At the end of the 1950s, the government, aware of the imminent termination of U.S. economic aid, started to prepare for the sudden withdrawal of massive foreign capital and material. Between 1958 and 1960, major policy reforms were instituted in the foreign exchange and tax system to encourage investments and savings. In essence, these reforms sought to remove structural barriers to economic development and to neutralize forces that interfered with market functions. As a result of these preparatory measures, the eventual termination of U.S. aid in 1965 did not bring economic growth to a halt as many had feared. Instead, the island's domestic savings, business investments, and exports experienced an enormous growth after 1965. Through these developments Taiwan had attained a new structure capable of promoting accelerated growth, which did in fact occur in the following decade. During this period, the economy averaged an annual growth rate of 10.2 percent, which put Taiwan in a select group with Japan as one of the few economies that had achieved an extremely high growth.

The rapid growth of the economy produced the long-awaited prosperity in Taiwan. Markets enjoyed plentiful supplies for the first time in many years, and the economy was no longer so vulnerable to inflation. The economic growth also increased productivity per unit of input, which effectively absorbed the pressure for wage increases that usually accompanies rapid economic growth. Thus, the cost per labor unit in the economy was actually reduced. Fortunately, prices on the international markets had also been stable. Being an island economy, Taiwan depends to a great extent on foreign trade; stable prices on the international markets contributed to stable prices on the domestic market. Thus, the cost-of-living increase was kept at a low 3.3 percent annual rate. This was one of the rare eras in recent history when the Taiwanese enjoyed rapid economic growth and low inflation at the same time.

The fourth economic development stage in Taiwan began in 1973 and extends to the present time. In 1973 the economy continued the high growth trend that had started in the previous decade and recorded a robust 12 percent annual growth rate. During that year, the U.S. dollar experienced a steep depreciation which disrupted the stability of the international monetary market. To worsen the situation, globalwide bad weather caused a worldwide low agricultural yield which affected supplies in the international food markets. In October of that year, war broke out in the Middle East, a global oil crisis was in the making, and the oil price on the international markets was on a steady rise. The oil price in Taiwan during the first two months of 1974 climbed 300 percent, triggering double digit inflation on the island. At the time, Taiwan had accrued a huge foreign trade surplus which soon developed into a wild money supply expansion. This situation fueled Taiwan's already bad inflation to a 27.8 percent annual rate.

Reacting to the rapidly escalating inflation, the government promptly reduced its expenditures. As Taiwan's oil price shot up, the expensiveness of the price itself forced a voluntary reduction of oil consumption. As a result, the price began to stabilize. On the international scene, as oil-producing countries kept raising oil prices, developed nations were forced to cut down their consumption in other categories to balance expenses. The resulting worldwide reduction of consumption adversely affected Taiwan's exports. The Taiwanese actually welcomed this slide in performance, for it relieved them from the inflationary threat of an oversupply of money created by a too large trade surplus. The downward export trade performance actually rescued the economy from a potentially high inflation.

Although Taiwanese economists welcomed the check on the country's exports, the slowdown in the growth of exports aroused wide concern among the public about the future of the economy. This concern was soon reflected in the public's lack of interest in business investments, a problem that could have a serious effect on economic growth. To counteract the economy's apparent tendency toward recession, in 1974 the government began to implement in full force a series of major public construction and industrial projects in the hope of injecting the growth impetus needed for a total revitalization.[8] Later, a number of policy measures were also instituted to stimulate the economy, such as those aimed at lowering the interest rate to encourage investment borrowings. The economy responded well to the revitalization and stimulation measures. In 1976 the economy registered an annual growth rate of 13.5 percent, and in the following year, the rate was even higher, 13.9 percent.

In 1979 the war between Iran and Iraq broke out, again causing the world oil price to skyrocket, and once again Taiwan's economy was badly affected by it. The growth of the economy in 1979 and 1980 had reached an annual rate of only 7.4 percent. In 1984 a somewhat improved international economic condition helped expand Taiwan's exports, the economic growth rate of that year reached 10.9 percent, and in 1986 the rate increased to 11.6 percent. During these last four years, Taiwan was under heavy pressure to voluntarily restrain its exports to the United States. In the meantime, the value of its currency experienced a 40 percent appreciation against the U.S. dollar. These two developments seriously threatened to bankrupt most of its export industries.[9]

Economists in Taiwan noted that the island's high rate of savings had been an important factor in its development success. They attributed the obvious low rate of savings of the island's economy during its early development stage to the very low per capita income earned during that period. Between 1953 and 1960, the ratio of savings to GNP was only 10 percent; the savings accounted for only 60 percent of total investment needs, with U.S. economic aid supplementing most of the unmet capital needs. To promote savings, in 1960 the government launched a nationwide campaign to persuade all its people to participate in savings programs. This was one of the government's many well-received policy measures designed to overcome obstacles to economic development. The public's response to the campaign was a total fulfillment of the government's campaign goal; the rate of savings on the island increased immensely as

a result. At the time U.S. economic aid ended in 1965, the island was able
to generate 86 percent of its investment needs. During 1970 again the ratio
of savings to GNP was as high as 30 percent. Thus, Taiwan had successfully broken the vicious cycle that usually plagued the economy of poor
countries: low per capita income generates low savings, which is responsible for low business investments, which leads back to low per capita
income.[10]

Taiwan's economic achievements go beyond what impressive statistical
figures can convey. Through the years a more mature and strengthened
economic structure capable of taking on a faster paced and even more
ambitious economic growth in the future evolved on the island. In the last
forty years, Taiwan has successfully completed a transition from an
agricultural economy of the early days to the present industrial economy.
Today, over half of Taiwan's industrial products are credited to the heavy
and chemical sector of the industry, which represents a big shift from the
predominance of the labor-intensive industry back in the 1960s. Although
the current composition of Taiwan's industry does not measure up to what
it is in the developed economies, it appears to have a healthy structural
foundation capable of full development. In 1952 Taiwan's agricultural
products accounted for 36 percent of domestic gross products, whereas
industrial products made up 18 percent. Not until 1963 did the ratio of
industrial products to domestic gross products for the first time surpass
that held for agricultural products, 28 percent and 27 percent, respectively.
In 1987 agricultural products made up only 6.6 percent of Taiwan's
domestic gross products, and among industrial outputs, 44.5 percent were
categorized as labor intensive and 55.5 percent as heavy or chemical. In
1980 the government targeted nine high tech areas for rapid intensive
development—energy, material science, information, manufacturing automation, laser technology, genetic engineering, biological technology, and
food technology. Since then the Taiwanese have made immense progress
in these areas.

Although Taiwan is rightfully proud of its economic accomplishments,
equally commendable has been its ability to keep the inflation rate low as
well as to effect an equal distribution of income when the economy was
experiencing unprecedented prosperity. Older Chinese in Taiwan know all
too well the deadly effect of inflation; they witnessed the chaos created by
rampant inflation at the end of World War II which cost the Nationalist
government the mainland. At one time that inflation ran as high as 1600
percent a year. For the next three years after the Nationalist government
resettled on Taiwan, it devoted much of its energies to fighting inflation.
In 1949 the government implemented a currency reform in the vain hope

of controlling inflation. It adopted a number of anti-inflation measures—a high interest policy to absorb uncommitted capital, use of gold to guarantee the value of bank deposits against the dissipating effect of inflation, and an islandwide prince control. A total of three and half years elapsed before the measures began to show steady results: in 1953 inflation dropped from 1600 to 62 percent per year. The government's postwar restoration efforts had raised agricultural and industrial production to its prewar level. That effectively controlled the major cause of the inflation— the shortage of material supplies.

In 1953 the first of a series of economic plans was inaugurated. In this plan a stable economy was considered to be as important as the ultimate goal—promotion of the island's economic growth. From 1961 to 1972, this dual emphasis produced the lowest inflation rate since the government had relocated: it averaged 3.3 percent per year. Local economists attributed this accomplishment to four forces: (1) the overall stability of the global economy and the plentiful products supply in international markets, (2) the high quality of Taiwan's labor force which contributed to a low per unit labor cost, (3) the high savings rate, and (4) the balanced budget.[11]

The period of low inflation rates finally ended in 1973. In that year, the international market price for agricultural commodities shot up owing to a poor harvest; Taiwan, which depended on sizable agricultural imports each year to satisfy its domestic consumption needs, was therefore affected. In the same year, the Middle East war sent Taiwan's oil price up 300 percent. Taiwan's economy was directly affected by these two international developments. Its inflation rate climbed up 47 percent during the year. This time, however, the Taiwanese were quick to adopt effective inflation control measures, and so the inflation was contained in two years. When Taiwan was hit by the second oil crisis in 1979, its inflation rate was a much tamed annual rate of 22 percent. In 1982, after a currency supply control policy was instituted, the inflation was reduced to an annual rate of 3 percent. Yet, oversupply of currencies remained a persistent problem. Many believe the problem occurred because the government had held a large amount of foreign currency reserves over a long period of time. As of the last count, Taiwan had foreign currency reserves of U.S. $74 billion.

Economic equality has been a very important issue in the political history of contemporary China. Many historians believe that this very issue permitted the rise of the Chinese Communists and was responsible for the ultimate defeat of the Nationalists in 1949. For this reason, from the beginning of its rule on Taiwan the Nationalist government was determined to advocate a policy of equal distribution of income. According to a study conducted by the U.S. Overseas Development Council, the income disparity between the richest and the poorest in Taiwan has been closing up steadily in spite of the island's economic growth—from 15 times in 1950 to 4.5 times in 1989 in comparison with 9.5 times in the United States, 6.5 times in West Germany, and 5.4 times in Great Britain.

Taiwan's achievements in economic equality may be attributed to a number of policies. First, the country's land reforms greatly contributed to the equalization of wealth among its farming population. Between 1949 and 1953, a series of progressive land reform measures were implemented regulating the farmland rentals to no higher than 37.5 percent of the total annual land yields; selling state-owned lands to landless farmers; and restricting the ownership of farmlands to working farmers to eliminate absentee landlordships. The land reforms not only achieved equalization of farmland, but also greatly boosted the farmers' working morale and production incentives. These changes increased production and income on the farm. In 1972 the government launched a large-scale agricultural infrastructure construction program designed to speed up agricultural growth. In addition, the government purchasing guaranteed program ensured a total purchase of the farmers' products at prices profitable to them. Furthermore, improved and expanded transportation between the countryside and the cities helped to bring businesses and industries to the countryside, which also had beneficial effects, narrowing the income gap between urban and rural areas.

Second, the policy to develop labor-intensive industries during the 1960s created abundant jobs for nonskilled labor, thus largely reducing the unemployment rate among the low-income population. In addition, since labor-intensive industrial enterprises in Taiwan were extremely lucrative at the time and the financial and technical requirements for establishing such businesses were not demanding, a large number of skilled labor workers started their own businesses, thus making an upward move to the upper middle class.

Third, education was made extremely accessible financially and geographically to all who sought to improve their economic opportunities. In particular, quality vocational education enabled those at the bottom of the economic echelon to obtain higher earning jobs. Between 1953 and 1983, the number of children attending school increased by 4.3 percent, which was higher than the growth in the island's birth rate, 2.7 percent. In the last five years, the number of schooled children reached 99 percent of the total school-aged children.

Finally, the progressive income tax system was instrumental in equalizing the distribution of income among the Taiwanese. The recent government attempt to tighten up tax collections to reduce evasion, to adjust tax rates to increase the tax responsibilities of the high-income group, and to reduce the tax burdens of the low-income population should help advance this goal.

In summary, what started forty-one years ago on Taiwan as an effort to restore its war-ruined economy and to increase production to meet the basic needs of its people evolved into a successful development example for the Third World economies. The economic development effort progressed in four stages: import substitution, export expansion, promotion of heavy and petrochemical industries, and development of high tech industries, which transformed the island from a traditionally agricultural society to a modern industrial society. While Taiwan was experiencing an unprecedented rapid economic growth, the Taiwanese were able to attend to their commitment to equalizing income distribution as well as to creating a modern economic structure that would support the free operation of the market functions and allow the economy to advance to its next level of growth.

NOTES

1. Ching-Yuan Lin, *Industrialization in Taiwan, 1946–1972* (New York: Praeger, 1973).

2. Tso-Yuong Wang, *Economic Miracle* (Taipei: Time Publishing Co., 1984), p. 8.

3. Executive Yuan, Council on Economic Development, *The Journey of the Modernization of Taiwan's Economy* (Taipei: Bureau of Economic Research, 1987), p. 25.

4. For sources on Taiwan's colonial economy, see Department of Economic Research, Bank of Taiwan, *Taiwan Economic Development Research* (Taipei: Bank of Taiwan Press, 1970); Ho Sam, *Economic Development of Taiwan, 1860–1970* (New Haven, Conn.: Yale University Press, 1978); and George Barclay, *Colonial Development and Population in Taiwan* (Port Washington, N.Y.: Kennikat Press, 1972).

5. For a detailed report on Taiwan's early industrial development, see Wen-Pau Chang, "Industrialization of the Last Sixteen Years," in *Taiwan Economic Development Research* (Taipei: Bank of Taiwan Press, 1970), pp. 266–282.

6. 1990 Taiwan Data Book.

7. The figure was given by Minister Kwoh-Ting Li.

8. A number of these projects had actually already started at an earlier time, although on a much smaller scale and at a slower rate.

9. For the source on the four stages of economic development on Taiwan, see Executive Yuan, *The Journey of the Modernization of Taiwan's Economy*.

10. For a detailed report on the savings of Taiwan's economy, see Chiang-Sian Wang, "Finance in Taiwan of the Last Sixteen Years," in *Taiwan Economic Development Research* (Taipei: Bank of Taiwan Press, 1970), pp. 138–163.

11. Executive Yuan, *The Journey of the Modernization of Taiwan's Economy*, p. 16.

3 A CENTURY OF PREPARATION FOR MODERN ECONOMIC GROWTH

It took China a total century, from 1849, the year it opened its doors to foreign influence, to 1949 when the Nationalist government relocated to Taiwan, to prepare for modern economic growth. Ironically, this long-awaited transition finally took place when the Nationalist Chinese were in exile on the island of Taiwan where conditions had availed themselves to such a move, and the Chinese, after a century of preparation, were capable of launching the island's economy for a giant leap forward. The century-long transformation process the country underwent represents a series of social and cultural revolutions in which obstructive elements of the social and cultural structure to modern economic growth were removed and favorable ones installed. The evolution was intriguingly complex, yet determinedly purposeful, leading to the country's complete transformation from a stagnant, tradition-laden agrarian society to one equipped with modern structures ready to advance to the modern age. The apparent forcefulness, determination, and purposefulness of this process suggest that the evolution was more than a result of plans or visions of individual leaders in history. It could only come from the powerful inner strength of a culture that was struggling to preserve its existence in human history.

This chapter examines China's social and cultural evolution based on the assumption that China's transition to modernity was historically inevitable and that the grave challenges which modern Western civilization had presented at the time was a necessary stimulus to effect this gigantic shift in Chinese culture and society.

The history of China during this one hundred-year period can be read as a series of vast, turbulent, often violent changes that took place in response to the unprecedented challenges posed by the modern age. In the political arena, the Chinese people's quest for modern political structure and institutions brought about a number of major changes—the Restoration Movement of Emperor Tongzhi which lasted from 1862 to 1874, the Reformist Movement which began in 1895, the new political system, the constitutional monarchy during the last few years of the Ching Dynasty, the revolution that led to the founding of the Republic of China in 1911, and the decades of ideological rivalry between the Nationalists and the Communists which ended in a division of China in 1949.

To make the Chinese language suitable for science, modern technology, international business, and other modern applications, the traditional literary style of the language gave way to a form of conversational language, a result of the New Language Movement of 1919. To teach the sciences, technology, foreign history, literature, and other modern subjects of learning in China, a Western educational system was established to replace the centuries-old private tutor instruction which only the well-to-do could afford, and a compulsory public education was widely enforced in the country.[1] Foreign trade and Western influence in China gave rise to a new social class which consisted primarily of foreign trade merchants, industrialists, and Western-educated scholars and officials. Compelled by their newly acquired modern views, and as the enlightened citizens in an old country, they felt it was their responsibility to bring the country to modernity.

Obviously overwhelmed by what they perceived to be the awesome superiority of Western technology, the Chinese began a long, hard critical examination of their society and culture in a solemn attempt to transform the society and culture, making them capable of meeting modern challenges. Understandably, throughout the transitional period tensions arose between forces fighting to retain the country's traditions and those championing a full emulation of Western scientific and technological advancements. Contrary to popular belief that when East meets West the traditional culture would totally give way to Western influences, the changes that took place did not indicate a wholesale adoption of Western civilization. Instead, the end product of the century-long adaptation and transformation was a modern social and cultural structure uniquely Chinese, yet supportive of the country's drive for modern economic growth.

Removing the structural obstacles to modern economic growth was an essential accomplishment of the adaptation and transformation. The primary obstacle was the absence in the Chinese culture of an ideology that would encourage and support profitmaking. In fact, the traditional Chinese culture attached negative values to material well-being and technological advancements. The plentiful supply of manual labor, the static, closed stratification structure, the admiration of frugality, and the contempt for material consumption in the traditional China all had negative impacts on the profitmaking motive of the Chinese and their pursuit of material well-being and technological advancements.

The rich manpower resource in the traditional China actually became an impediment to progress in an age of mechanization, and the vast Chinese population did not translate into a large consumer market capable of sustaining a manufacturing industry. On the contrary, the traditional Chinese culture, where motivation for material well-being and upward social mobility was low, had only turned China's vast population into a rich supply of manual labor, obliterating any real need for mechanization. Therefore, China began to appreciate technology only in the mid-nineteenth century when it confronted the Western military might for the first time and was thus shockingly awakened to the urgent need to build its military technology. China's first modernization plan, which was implemented in the mid-nineteenth century, was, in fact, designed to build shipyards and arsenals. The Chinese adopted consumer manufacturing only after the Westerners' manufacturing plants in China had produced low-cost, large-volume products and had shown their remarkable advantages in the marketplace over locally handmade products.[2]

The Chinese economy failed to achieve production mechanization during its own course of evolution, despite its potentially huge consumer market. The reason also had to do with the market demand end of the economy. Frugality and restraint of material consumption were the basic characteristics of the Chinese. Moreover, the ability to withstand material temptation was an important consideration in China for appointments to high government offices. Therefore, it has been a common practice among the people in high offices as well as China's community leaders to publicly display these virtues. In addition, the Chinese concept of diligence might have also been working against the idea of production mechanization, for the Chinese tended to associate diligence with manual labor and long working hours. Suggestions for cutting down production time at traditional Chinese workplaces may be regarded as the lazy workers' attempts to have an easier time at work. Furthermore, the Chinese culture's natural tendency to preserve traditions and to resist changes might have constituted formidable obstacles to technological advancements in China. Chinese artisans and craftsmen took pride in inheriting, preserving, and handing down trade skills that had been in the family for generations. In addition, the traditional

Chinese consumers desired and trusted products made with centuries-old secret craft skills.

The static stratification structure and the resulting lack of social mobility in traditional Chinese society may also have had some negative impacts on the profitmaking motivation. As a purposeful human activity, profit-making should be a means to fulfill some goals that carry high values to the doer. Clearly, no ideology such as the Protestant work ethic, which provided the fundamental motivation for profitmaking activities among sixteenth-century Calvinists, had been present in the Chinese culture. In fact, the Chinese culture despised moneymaking as petty and "unclean," for, in the view of the Chinese, it often involved dishonesty and taking advantage of others. Because of the static nature of Chinese society, profitmaking was hardly a means to improve one's social standing. Social stratification was based not on one's birth, but rather on a hierarchy of classes of occupation which appeared in a descending order as follows: scholars, farmers, laborers, and merchants. Associations between people across social boundaries were discouraged. People who owned capital, such as the scholar-mandarins, for example, did not engage in business adventures with people who owned production skills such as the laborers, peddlers, or shop owners. In the absence of banking systems, people of lower social classes did not have access to large business capital. There-fore, ordinary people were severely limited in their ability to make big profits in business that would earn them enough power to launch a revolt against the established order, as did the sixteenth-century merchants in European cities. Yet, within the static stratification structure, acquired wealth alone hardly afforded people higher social status. Being at the bottom of the static social hierarchy, Chinese merchants did not regard profitmaking as an effective means to improve their social standing.

Talent and energy in traditional Chinese society were channeled into activities other than economic ones. The growth and vitality of an econ-omy, depends, to a large extent, on the society's reward system. In traditional Chinese society those with the greatest talents had long been attracted to membership in the ruling class, the scholar-mandarin, for this class owned well-protected sources of wealth, held enormous social and political power, and commanded unchallenged respect. Since the Chin Dynasty, whose reign in China began in the latter part of the fourth century, an elaborately structured and administered imperial examination system had been in place for selecting among mass contestants a small number of people each year based on literary ability. Those deemed worthy of various grades of titles of scholar became qualified for high imperial offices. The examination was open to everyone, regardless of birth or race origin, and tested the contestants' knowledge of Chinese classics covering the subject areas of history, literature, political philosophy, and ethics.

The Chinese believed that superior personal qualities, such as genuine commitment to the public welfare, propriety, a superior sense of justice, and self-denial, were required of the successful imperial official. It was thought that diligently studying and meditating on the Chinese classics was a sure way to develop these qualities. Therefore, those who in the imperial examinations proved to have a superior command of the Chinese classics were said to possess supreme personal qualities. This selection practice was in use for centuries and was not abolished until the end of the nineteenth century when the Chinese recognized that the contents of the examination were irrelevant to one's ability to perform government duties.

Because the route to becoming a scholar-mandarin via the imperial examination was a socially acclaimed path to wealth and fame, it attracted the brightest, most talented, and most ambitious people. The imperial examination system consisted of a series of examinations; the contestants needed to pass a lower level in order to go on to the next level. It usually took several years of preparation between levels. Therefore, preparing for the examination could consume a good part of the contestant's life. However, as noted above, the system selected only a small number of superior performers who would be awarded the title of scholar. At some point in the examination system, the majority of the contestants were disqualified from becoming scholar-mandarins. Yet, those who entered the contest and were disqualified in the process had already studied for the examination for years. They themselves as well as the society identified them as members of the intelligentsia, and they were socially discouraged from engaging in manual labor or trade. Thus, those who tried and failed lost not only the most productive years of their lives in preparing for the examination, but by identifying with the intelligentsia in the process of study they also disassociated themselves from any form of manual productive labor. Being the most prominent reward system in traditional China, the imperial examination system was actually very counterproductive to economic progress.

The Chinese imperial government failed to assume an active role in the economic life of the people who, by tradition, were accustomed to looking to the state for guidance in nearly every aspect of life. Throughout the history of imperial China, the state's primary responsibility was twofold: to defend the sovereignty and its standing with its vassalage in international relations, and to secure stability and harmony within the empire. History indicates that the Chinese emperor and his government were subjected to the critical judgments of their subjects mostly in their ability to maintain the empire's honorable standing in the international community and to control corruption within government. The biggest threat to a Chinese dynasty was the occurrence of natural catastrophes such as famines which in China were usually caused by floods. The Chinese interpreted natural catastrophes as signs of heavenly displeasure with the dynasty in power. Ill-managed relief work of natural catastrophes could spawn unrest and develop into revolts against the dynasty. In fact, changes of dynasty in China can often be traced to such an origin. To prevent famines, Chinese emperors were particularly attentive to the construction and maintenance of rivers and dikes.

This attention was perhaps as close to becoming involved in the economic life of the people as the Chinese emperors ever come. The Chinese completely failed to see that the state had any role in economy; as a result they did not demand economic leadership of the state. Furthermore, in Chinese folk religions heaven controls all good and bad things that happen in life, be they the birth or the sex of babies, performance in the imperial examination, health, safe journey, crop harvest, and business success. Economic hardship was regarded as falling out of favor with heaven and was attributed to the failure of one's ancestors to do good deeds in life or being in discord with the forces of nature. With this line of belief prevalent, the state was completely relieved of any responsibility for the economic condition of its people.

The corrupt administration of the imperial tax collection system in China alienated the people from the state. The German sociologist, Max Weber, contended that the complexity and enormity of collecting taxes in imperial China gave birth to the notorious Chinese bureaucracy. Whether or not we agree with Weber's interpretation, tax collection certainly appeared to be the single most important activity of the imperial Chinese government, while the ability to pay taxes was the single most troublesome financial concern in the life of the ordinary Chinese people. Tax assessments and collections had often been tainted with corruption and injustice. China's vast land and huge population made tax assessment and collection extremely difficult. Further complicating the task was the fact that there were a variety of taxes and they had to be collected by different levels of government. In addition to the more usual kind of taxes on property, income, sales, and inheritance, the people were subjected to a salt tax, slaughter tax, a tax on consumption oils, a production tax, tax on commodities, and others.

Both the imperial government and local governments were involved in tax assessment and tax collection. Some officials in China were actually compensated by a certain percentage of tax collected from their administrative areas. These practices led to corruption and injustice and made it difficult for offenders to be caught and convicted. To make up for tax revenues lost to the wide spread corruption, heavy taxes were levied, which often left the people destitute. Centuries of such corruption in the tax system bred a deep-seated mistrust of government among people who opted to conceal their business activities from the government for fear of opening the door to ruthless extortion or exorbitant tax rates which would lead them to bankruptcy.

The centuries-old bitter contentions in China between regional powers and the central government for the allegiance of the people and the control of local affairs made it impossible to provide centrally planned, unified economic development programs. Furthermore, deep-rooted antagonisms among regional forces precluded economic cooperation among regions, and often cross-regional trades were halted owing to regional feuds. In China, dialects, customs, and local political traditions bound together people who claimed an ancestral root in a common region. A common origin of ancestral root bred a special sense of belonging and loyalty; therefore, ordinary Chinese concerned themselves with only local issues. Chinese regionalism was reinforced by the fact that the local government or sometimes the resident military force ruled over people's lives with an almost unchecked power, which often overrode the order of the imperial government. Local governments levied sales, commodity, and other forms of taxes; they functioned as independent entities and negotiated among themselves tax privileges and trade barriers. An often applied trade barrier was the transit tax which was levied for transporting goods through a region. These practices adversely affected the free flow of commodities, thus fostering isolated, monopolized markets in China.

The Chinese value system, institutions, and social structure created formidable obstacles to modern growth. It was not until the nineteenth century that China was confronted with the challenges of the West and was forced into taking a hard reexamination of its values, culture, and social structure. Only then did changes begin to take place.

In the nineteenth century rapid, violent changes were charactertistic of almost every aspect of Chinese life. Technology and democracy were the two foremost products of Western civilization which China chose to borrow in its modernization effort during this period. The Chinese first came to know the superiority of Western technology following a series of military encounters with Western forces in the late nineteenth century. Once the Chinese opened their minds to the values of Western technology, they quickly adopted fundamental changes in their culture and society to enable a mass transplant of the technology into China. Foreign advisers were hired to teach the technology, students were sent abroad to pursue higher levels of study of science and technology, and delegations were dispatched to the West to search out examples of technology that could be duplicated at home. Modern battleship building and arsenals were among China's first adopted Western technologies. Western capital and technology were brought in to build railroads, telephone and telegram communication systems, and other modern facilities. Increased financial transactions with foreign banks necessitated the establishment of modern financial institutions.

The opening of Chinese ports to foreign trade spawned a new class of Westernized entrepreneurs and businessmen. Through them, Western business ideas and practices, and, most importantly, a positive attitude toward profitmaking were introduced and spread to the society. The fact that many renowned families entered into business, such as the Soongs and the Kungs, broke the centuries-old taboo against such a move by the social elites. Thus, it became possible for the rich financial and personnel resources held by the Chinese elite families to be channeled into economic activities. In the meantime, Western-educated scholars were recruited into the young Nationalist government and were put in charge of economic development activities such as railroad construction, mining, shipbuilding, and other high tech areas of the age. Their work exemplified the social desirableness of the economic applications of scholarship. This was a brand-new concept to the Chinese, and it was profoundly important to their modern economic growth.

Increased contacts with foreigners and exposure to foreign mass media introduced the Western way of life to China. Soon foreign-made products became a status symbol, and the number of importers and department stores that carried foreign products began to grow. In large cities, consumer markets for foreign-made products as well as products affording modern convenience swelled. At first, criticisms of the Western way of life as wasteful, vain, and corrupting to the soul were rampant. As modern conveniences spread to the countryside, however, more and more people subscribed to this new way of living, and the criticisms began to subside. This change in attitude greatly enhanced consumer demand in the marketplace and, therefore, greatly encouraged economic activities in China.

In addition to Western technology, after the Opium War the Chinese also sought to establish democracy for their country. Western democratic thought was first introduced into China by intellectuals who had studied abroad. As a major effort to spread democratic thought in China, many of the great philosophers of the time including John Dewey and Bertrand Russell were invited to China for a nationwide university speech tour. The revolutionary movement that toppled the Chinese dynasty in 1911 was formed and supported by Western-educated intellectuals. This started the unique leadership role of the Chinese intellectuals in championing major social and political movements in modern China. They played an essential part in the long war against the warlords which began in 1928, in the Nationalist government's declaration of war against Japanese aggressions which resulted in China's participation in World War II, in the introduction of communism to China, and in the student pro-democracy movement of the 1980s.

The political ideology, embodied in what was later called the Three Principles for the People (nationalism, democracy, and livelihood, which had inspired the Chinese revolution), was an ingenious blend of Western social and political thoughts and Chinese traditional philosophy. Among many other enlightening effects on the traditional Chinese, the ideology introduced the concept of the government's responsibility and accountability to its people, the value of political, social, and economic equality, and the importance of participatory democracy. At the time these ideas were fundamentally important to China's search for democracy.

The Three Principles for the People became the guiding political ideology of the Nationalist government during its rule both on the mainland and Taiwan. The ideology has been credited for Taiwan's economic success in at least two separate ways. First, the ideology inspired a strong sense of nationalism to support economic development efforts in Taiwan. As any ideology such as this one appeals to values and emotions of such a high level in the mental makeup of a nation, it always strengthens group solidarity and enables people to sustain themselves in difficult times. Dr. Sun Yat-Sen challenged the Chinese to eradicate the widespread poverty and backwardness in their country as the fundamental step to nation building. In order to resist the foreign aggressions which were seriously threatening China's sovereignty, he proposed a grand-scale nation-building plan, for in his view a wealthy and strong China was the best deterrent to such aggressions. He emphasized that modern technology and physical sciences were tools to this end. Thus, patriotism and a sense of national pride were injected into economic development. To this day, the nationalistic element in economic endeavors remains very much alive on Taiwan. Undoubtedly, nationalism may help explain the Taiwanese government officials' unusual level of commitment and determination to economic development efforts and the high degree of enthusiasm invested by Taiwanese businessmen in international trade.

Second, the theory of democracy in Dr. Sun Yat-Sen's Three Principles for the People encouraged the Chinese in the low social echelon to advance economically. In seeking individual economic welfare, they significantly contributed to their country's economic success. Lacking opportunities to change their economic standing, the Chinese at the bottom of society had traditionally been apathetic. Not only did Dr. Sun's theory of democracy reaffirm the right of all people to economic progress, but also in his theory of livelihood, one of three major books on this political thought, he stressed the concept of equal income. This concept primarily advocated the control of excessive wealth of the rich and the obligation to provide social and economic welfare to the poor. Later, the Chinese Communists' effective campaigns to organize the revolt of the poor forced the Chinese government to take seriously its responsibility to the deprived.

Decades of rivalry with the Chinese Communists made the Nationalist government more sensitive to its political, if not ideological, need to attend to the needs of its poor and powerless. Before relocating to Taiwan, the Nationalist government launched a series of social programs in designated regions on the mainland to improve the regime's economic equality. For example, in the 1930s, the president of Taiwan, Chiang Chien-Kuo, as a high-ranking Nationalist party official, led a successful implementation of a prototype land reform program in the Province of Chiensee to redistribute farmland to landless farmers. On Taiwan, the Nationalist government, throughout its entire economic development process, has stressed its commitment to an equalized distribution of income. Policies aimed at promoting economic growth have often been designed with built-in measures to effect economic equality. For example, the land reform program implemented in the late 1940s and early 1950s on Taiwan redistributed the island's farmland, giving the farmers greater incentive to increase production and income.

In the late 1950s, the government faced an economic development choice between promoting heavy industries and concentrating on the development of labor-intensive industries. The government chose the latter to create more jobs for the island's factory workers. For example, the government directed the small- and medium-sized labor-intensive industries to set up plants in the rural areas, thereby providing jobs for the surplus rural labor forces. In the 1960s a series of tax incentive programs were instituted to encourage small- and medium-sized enterprises; their existence had a profound effect on equalizing income.[3]

While Chinese culture was undergoing fundamental changes in values, thoughts, and attitude in preparation for modern economic growth, the Chinese social structure was also experiencing a rapid transformation in its march toward modernity. Because the 1911 revolution which overthrew the Ching Dynasty and established the republic was achieved without much bloodshed, most of the traditional Chinese political structure was left untouched. Except for the high-level administration in the newly formed central government, personnel and administrative practices in the new government remained as they were under the previous imperial rule. At the regional level, military strongmen controlled every aspect of the regional administration, and their rule was independent of that of the central government, an unfortunate legacy of the weak imperial government of the Ching Dynasty. Since their powers had lent support to the founding of the republic, the leaders of the regional forces believed that together they held the scale of power capable of tipping over the new government. The existence of these independent, strong regional forces and the contending, unstable political relationships between them and the central government made it easy for aggressive foreign powers to make advances in China. The advances made by Japan in Manchuria and northern China preceding the last Sino-Japanese War are good examples. The deeply divided administrative power in China incapacitated the central government to launch any unified, coordinated economic development programs in the country. For the first quarter of the twentieth century, the Nationalist government committed its resources and energies to wars to battle opposing regional forces.

Retaining the personnel and practices of the previous imperial government helped perpetuate the two most tenacious evils of traditional Chinese administration, corruption and ineffectiveness. Newly established private enterprises were, without exception, infected with these problems. The deep roots of these problems into the Chinese administrative structure and practices, and the magnitude of its spread to the country's organizations, made it almost impossible to correct the problems. Some leaders who were determined to eradicate these problems were convinced that the only solution was a total reconstruction of the Chinese personality. Recognizing the enormity of this task, later, the Chinese Communists believed that only a second revolution could thoroughly purge these and other deep-seated social illnesses and allow the new person and new society in the ideal image of communism to emerge. In 1926 Chiang Kai-Shek, or the Generalissimo as he was known, launched a nationwide character-rebuilding campaign, the New Life Movement. The movement was designed to cultivate a new set of moral values and behavioral patterns appropriate to modern society, including specific corrective prescriptions for those traditional behaviors and practices that perpetuated corruption and ineffectiveness. Although it is difficult to measure the result of these attempts to remold the Chinese character, it is at least clear that today Taiwan suffers these two problems only to the same degree as any other modern industrial society.

During the first thirty-eight years of the Chinese republic, the period prior to the Nationalist government's relocation to Taiwan, progress was made in many areas with respect to creating a social and institutional environment in China favorable to modern economic growth. For example, modern transportation and communications were established. Great strides were made in commerce, import and export trades were on the rise, and the first modern Chinese banking institute, the Central Bank, was founded. The first mission of the Bank was to unify the nation's currency and rationally manage foreign debts. Under the government's encouragement, labor unions were established to protect the workers' interests, and chambers of commerce were founded to promote business. In rural areas, agricultural experimentation stations and research organizations were founded, crop and breeding improvement programs were instituted, and agricultural educational projects were launched. Remarkable progress was made in education. A department of education was added to the central government structure to guide and enforce the quality of education. Equal educational opportunities were extended to girls and rural residents. Vocational education institutes were founded to provide training in technical and business skills. The subject matter at all levels of education began to incorporate scientific methods to problem solving. In the human resources arena, important progress was made in public health, equality for women, famine relief, and other social welfare areas.[4]

The relocation of the Nationalist government to Taiwan marked an important turning point in preparing Chinese society for modern economic growth. At least in four areas, conditions were more favorable for large-scale economic development efforts in Taiwan then on the mainland. First, the island is of course, much smaller than the mainland; Taiwan is about the size of Rhode Island whereas mainland China is comparable to the United States in size. Vast land and underdeveloped transportation on the mainland made it extremely difficult to effectively implement economic development programs. Prior to the relocation, economic development was unevenly distributed in China. In the coastal cities, both international and domestic commerce experienced rapid growth, and many modern infrastructures were already in place, whereas the inland economy suffered from slow development and underdeveloped infrastructures. In contrast, on Taiwan, the transportation and communications systems built during the Japanese colonial period established a good foundation for the economic development efforts of the Nationalist government. A central railroad connected the north end of the island to its south end, some regional railroads provided transportation between the west coast and the east coast, and highways reached to the countryside and remote areas. The island's airports and harbors provided sufficient international transport services. Mass media including newspapers and radio broadcasting reached every corner of the island.

Second, during the early Nationalist rule in Taiwan the vast majority of government officials came from the mainland; they had no political ties with the local powers. Moreover, after half a century of Japanese rule, there were few local Taiwanese political powers. As a result, the island's economic development programs were able to proceed without much opposition from organized local powers. Many Taiwan observers pointed out that the success of land reforms owed much to the fact that there was no organized opposition from landowners.

Third, the relocation of the government also helped reduce government corruption and ineffectiveness. The government employees who relocated from the mainland brought with them only their immediate families. They had no clans in Taiwan to whom they felt obliged, as was the Chinese custom, to care or provide employment for. Thus, the most common reason for corruption and nepotism was absent; no government jobs had to be created to provide employment for one's unqualified relatives. In the first few years following the government's relocation life was rather austere owing to postwar scarcity. In addition, the government was then fighting against the Communists' attempt to take over the island. As a result, a sense of urgency permeated the government. The combination of a generally austere material life and a sense of urgency probably generated voluntary restraints on the part of government employees from engaging in corruption and nepotism. Another explanation was that the government had relocated only the cream of the crop among the government employees.

Fourth, the government and the Taiwanese people were united in their commitment to and support for economic development efforts, for they all recognized that Taiwan was the last place to which the Nationalist government could retreat. The Communist regime on the mainland has never abandoned its claim on the island. The people on Taiwan, aware of the brutalities that took place during the Cultural Revolution on the mainland, knew what could happen to them should the island fall to the Communists. At the time of the relocation, both the government and the people saw the urgent need to reconstruct the island's economy to deter a Communist takeover. The common fight for survival united the people in the task of building a strong economy.

NOTES

1. For a detailed description of the changes that have taken place in China, consult Martin Kieffer, *The Awakening of China, 1793–1949* (New York: Putnam, 1967).

2. Jean Chesneaux, Marianne Bastid, and Marie-Claire Bergere, *China from the Opium Wars to the Nineteen Hundred Eleven Revolution* (New York: Pantheon, 1976) has a good account of the awakening of the Chinese to the value of technology and manufacturing.

3. For comprehensive coverage of the political ideology of Sun Yat-Sen, see Paul Lineborger, *The Political Doctrines of Sun Yat-Sen* (Baltimore: Johns Hopkins University Press, 1937).

4. Material on the modern construction of the early period of the Nationalist government come from Lloyd Eastman, *The Abortive Revolution: China Under Nationalist Rule, 1927–1937* (Cambridge, Mass.: Harvard University Press, 1974).

4 ECONOMIC DEVELOPMENT AND THE STRUGGLE FOR SURVIVAL

Nationalism is a major driving force behind economic development in Third World nations. It was nationalism that gave the Chinese the determination and commitment to improve their technology and overall economy. This determination and commitment is essential to an undertanding of Taiwan's economic success.

Chinese nationalism awakened the nineteenth-century Chinese to the challenges of modern times. This awakening represented the psychological turning point in China's long preparation for modern economic growth. China's nationalism was born of foreign aggressions. The Opium War began the period of foreign aggressions, and the surrender of the Japanese forces in China in 1945 marks the end of it. Nationalism embodied China's strong pride in its culture, the people's sense of oneness with their fellow countrymen, their love for their fatherland, and, most of all, their unique sense of mission as a nation.

Immediately following the Opium War, the fierce outrage of the Chinese over the British attempt to push opium sales to China through military force gradually, with the leadership of the intelligentsia, grew into an all-out effort to bring technology and democracy to China. This would be the nation's counterstrategy to secure its survival in the midst of Western aggressions. Later, Dr. Sun Yat-Sen, in his Three Principles for the People, ingeniously captured the national sentiment, gave it an ideological structure, and offered it as a firm psychological foundation for the Chinese commitment to a total social, political, and economic reconstruction of the country.

Japan's aggressions against China, especially those that occurred immediately before World War II, raised Chinese nationalism to its highest point. Japan's economic success had been both a painful stimulus and an encouragement to China's economic aspirations, for although Japan shares a similar cultural background, is located in the same global region, and comprises the same race of people as China, it succeeded in its economic development half a century before. The challenge of the Japanese success was more intensely felt by the people on Taiwan, for they had personally witnessed the economic accomplishments of the colonial Japanese. Postwar economic efforts on Taiwan were clearly mixed with a strong sense of nationalism. That nationalism gave rise to altruism, a high level of cooperation, an unselfish dedication, and a determination to overcome difficulties and strive for success. These qualities generally characterized men and women on the island who dedicated themselves to Taiwan's economic development activities.

Unlike the liberal nationalism which emerged in the United States and Western Europe in the eighteenth century, Chinese nationalism was born out of an urgent need in the mid-nineteenth century to preserve the people and culture in the face of concerted foreign attempts to colonize their country. Their history and culture bred in the Chinese a special sense of pride and mission as a people. When this pride was violated and the vision of their historical mission shattered, as happened during the foreign aggressions in the nineteenth century, Chinese nationalism was born. Isolated from the rest of the world, the ancient Chinese had developed an innocent view of themselves and others. They saw themselves as a people situated at the center of the universe, and from this unique cosmic location China derived its name. The word "China" means the "Central Kingdom," and the states that surrounded them were known as "barbarians," peoples whom the Chinese felt they had the moral obligation to teach and acculturate. This perception was further enforced by the lordship and vassal state relationship that had existed for centuries between China and its neighboring states, including what is today Korea, Vietnam, Thailand, Sikkim, and some Southeast Asian countries. As late as the nineteenth century, some of these countries still carried out their obligations as vassals, paying homage to China in exchange for military protection.

Seeing the world in this context of international relationships, Confucius (c. fifth century B.C.) developed a political philosophy with regard to the ultimate goal of humankind: the eternal peace of the world, and China's mission to carry out this goal. In Confucius' view, eternal world peace can be achieved only by appealing to the moral conscience of individuals. Therefore, China had the moral obligation to preach moral principles to the world. China itself would serve as a true practitioner of the moral principles, the worldwide practice of which would naturally lead to eternal world peace. The innocence of this view is apparent.

Many philosophers explained the naivete of the Chinese world-view as the product of a people who had lived for centuries isolated from the wars and aggressions of the rest of the world. It is therefore understandable that the Chinese, after having embraced such a worldview for thousands of years, were shocked by the West's aggression immediately before and after the Opium War. They were ashamed by their humiliating defeats by the West and by the unequal treaties forced on them after the wars. It is also from the perspective of this world-view that we can understand the magnanimous, unconditional forgiveness which Chiang Kai-Shek offered the Japanese at the end of World War II, absolving them of the atrocities and property damages in China during the war.

China's encounter with the West dates back to the seventeenth century when the Jesuits introduced Christianity to the land. The Jesuits were admitted to the imperial court during the last period of the Ming Dynasty and the succeeding Ching Dynasty. Their knowledge of mathematics, astronomy, cartography, and artillery, as well as their interest in translating Western scientific and technical works into Chinese, won them the trust of the Chinese. They were given official positions as astronomers, cartographers, and doctors. When the Napoleonic wars ended, the expansion of the Western economies drove traders to the Far East. The Chinese emperor's closed-door policy had discouraged Western attempts to establish formal trade relations with China. At the time, the Chinese imperial administrative structure did not include a Ministry of Foreign Relations or its equivalent; all matters relating to trade with foreigners were handled by local offices.

During the first half of the nineteenth century, purchases made by British and American firms in the southeastern parts of China multiplied. Increasingly anxious to balance their trade with China, the Westerners began smuggling opium into China where opium use was forbidden except for medical uses. According to Chinese estimates, 90 percent of Chinese officials became opium smokers, and nationwide, the number of opium smokers rose to 12 million. The magnitude of drug use compelled the imperial government to pass severe drug correction measures. The special commissioner, Lin Ze-Xu, who later became the central figure in the controversy that led to the Opium War, was sent to Canton, the southeastern coastal province, where most foreign trade was conducted, to clean out the opium smuggling. In Canton, the measures Lin took when he arrived in 1839 were aimed just as much at the Chinese accomplices and clients of the foreign firms as at the firms themselves. In two months, he made one thousand arrests and confiscated eleven thousand pounds of opium. Later, in June of that year, he forced factories to hand over about twenty thousand crates of smuggled opium and ordered them destroyed. From the Chinese point of view, the measures were aimed strictly at domestic drug use problems.

In response to these seizures, the British summoned their warships to Kwontzou, the capital city of Canton, and bombarded the port. The fight later spread to the region near the north of the Yangtze River where the British overcame the imperial troops with ease. This was the beginning of what would become known as the Opium War. The British attacks, especially following such a series of events, aroused violent reaction throughout China. Sporadic citizen-initiated and organized attacks were made on the British in places where they traded. The most serious incident occurred near a village in Canton, Sanyuanli where several thousand peasants armed with pikes, scythes, and bamboo rods surrounded an Anglo-Indian battalion that had been looting the countryside, desecrating tombs, and molesting women. In retaliation the British launched military attacks on several cities. Many other foreign powers with interests in China joined forces with Britain in these attacks.

In 1842 the conciliatory group of the Chinese imperial government negotiated treaties with the foreign powers involved in the Opium War. The Treaty of Nanking between China and Great Britain was signed in 1842, a supplementary treaty was signed in the following year, a treaty with France in 1844, and a treaty with the United States in the same year. These treaties forced China to open its doors to foreign commercial activities under conditions determined by these foreign powers. Some treaty terms concerning Britain only seriously increased that country's belligerent power in China. For example, the island of Hong Kong was ceded to Britain, the Chinese agreed to pay an indemnity of Mexican $21 million, and British troops were to occupy the Zhonsan Islands until the sum was handed out. The advantages which these treaties gave these foreign powers formed the basis of an unequal treaty system which would be developed during the remainder of the nineteenth century and the early twentieth century.[1]

The unequal treaties, together with the aggressive events that led up to them, profoundly shocked the Chinese and completely changed their way of thinking. Historians have observed that the Opium War marked the beginning of this Asian giant's awakening to the challenges and responsibilities of a nation in the modern era. After signing these treaties, the Chinese embarked on a long process of self-examination of their culture, institutions, and social structure in an urgent attempt to modernize their culture and nation. Two major nationwide efforts were attempted during the remaining years of the Ching Dynasty. Following the Opium War, the emperor was urged to speed up the transfer of Western military technology into China to help build a modern Chinese military force to defend the country against foreign aggressors. The first of these modernization attempts was a "self-strengthening movement" that lasted twelve years, from 1860 to 1872. During this period, China took several steps toward modernizing its military technology, produced imitation English guns and cannons, adopted new and improved shipbuiding technology, and founded several modern arsenals. In 1872 the second modernization attempt—this one dedicated to lift China to wealth and power—was inaugurated, and it was carried out through 1885. During this period, specialized commercial agriculture began to emerge in rural China, and modern business enterprises started to appear. In 1872 the China Merchants' Steam Navigation Company was founded. Mines were developed to meet the needs of the armaments and steam navigation industry, as well as to forestall foreigners from demanding the right to open mines in China. Private enterprises flourished, especially in the textile and silk industries. Major progress was made in communications—railroads, telegraph, and postal services were installed.[2]

The Ching Dynasty's failure to defend the empire against foreign aggressions sowed the seed for the Chinese revolution. The revolution gained its chief support from the country's young intellectuals and students who had been inspired by the nationalist ideology of the revolutionary leader, Dr. Sun Yat-Sen. During the revolution, they repeatedly exhibited their fearless willingness to give their lives for an independent, strong, prosperous China. Through wide popular support the revolution succeeded without much bloodshed. In the theory of livelihood, one of Sun Yat-Sen's Three Principles for the People, he explained why reconstructing the nation's economy would be an effective strategy in making China a strong nation. Through the proposed economic reconstruction and social welfare, the Chinese could be lifted out of poverty and ignorance and the newly established democracy could derive some actual operative meaning in China. By building national wealth, China's international standing could be restored. Finally, economic justice was a prerequisite to a stable and growing economy, essential to a strong China.[3]

While the Western aggressors awoke China to the urgency of fighting for its survival, China learned an ever harder lesson from the Japanese of the necessity to strengthen itself through economic development. China's rivalry with Japan beginning in the nineteenth century enhanced China's nationalism and strengthened its resolve to build the economy. Physical proximity had allowed a close cultural affinity between the two countries. The short physical distance between the two also gave rise to competition and conflict between them in more modern times. After the Meiji Restoration, Japan moved rapidly toward industrialization, which necessitated that the island country seek access to natural resources elsewhere. China became a natural target of this expansion effort. Japan had progressively built its influence and power in neighboring China where the Japanese found rich natural resources and a huge consumer market. The first Sino-Japanese War in 1895 awoke the Chinese to the Japanese expansion intent. At the end of the war, the weak and inept Ching Dynasty agreed to cede Taiwan to Japan. Shortly afterward, Japan stepped up its influence, expanding into Manchuria. From there, Japan expanded southward to the vicinity of the ancient capital city. During the years immediately preceding World War II, Japan's expansion into China presented the fearful prospect of China as a Japanese colony. In these years, however, China was rocked by civil war between the Nationalists and the Communists, and the country had just begun an all-out national reconstruction effort. Thus, China was in no position to wage a massive military resistance against the Japanese invasion. Even so, the fierce indignation of the Chinese public over Japan's military aggressions and atrocities aroused the Chinese nationalist spirit as never before. Young men quit schools in large numbers to join the military; young women became military nurses. Ordinary people turned in their jewelry and other precious possessions to help pay for the purchase of arms. The entire nation voluntarily mobilized to resist the Japanese. Finally, the Chinese people pleaded with their government to declare war with Japan. From 1937 to 1945, for eight years, the Chinese fought a long, hard war with Japan. Their severe losses and suffering during the war hardened the Chinese, making them determined to build a strong wealthy nation to deter future Japanese aggressions. When the Chinese Nationalist government relocated to Taiwan and found massive economic development works being accomplished on the island by the colonial Japanese, the government officials, vowed to produce an even better record on the island. Undoubtedly, Japan's brilliant postwar economic success and its rise to super economic power status were a great inspiration to the Taiwanese in their struggle to participate in the world economic scene.

Shortly after the Chinese Nationalist government relocated to Taiwan, the Chinese Communists made a real threat to take it over. By then, the Chinese Communists occupied the entire mainland and were ready to march across the ocean. On the island, the war-torn economy needed to be restored, and millions of new immigrants had to be fed and clothed. The circumstance presented an urgent need to build the island's economy.

The Nationalist government began a massive campaign to engage the schools, government offices, and the mass media in cultivating Nationalism and successively rooted a political ideology on economic development in the people. The pursuit of rapid economic growth and international trade expansion was an effective means to raise the island's international standing. Each major economic achievement reinforced the correctness of the government's chosen course and strengthened the people's determination to proceed. The government kept a close tally of each achievement and prepared regular reports that they compared to established international records. The newspapers headlined the economic performance, stimulating national pride. As a result, the nation's confidence rose, and government officials were hailed as national heroes. Taiwanese regard business success in the international market as an honorable way for citizens to fulfill their responsibility.

Today, neither the Nationalist government on Taiwan nor the Communist government on the mainland can ignore the ongoing force pushing for a unified China. In view of recent developments between the two Chinas in the direction of unity, the establishment of a joint council to arbitrate trading affairs between the two peoples, the approval of tourist visits and limited immigration to the other China, and mail and telephone communications across the straits, it is not unreasonable to speculate that the two Chinas may indeed soon come together. Taiwan's capital and technology can, of course, measurably promote mainland China's economy, while the huge consumer market and rich natural resources of the mainland offer a growth alternative much needed by Taiwan.

Taiwan's prosperity has significantly raised its international standing. Today, without the benefit of diplomatic recognition by most of the world, Taiwan has been able to advance its international visibility by increasingly participating in international organizations and activities. Currently, Taiwan offers economic development and humanitarian aid to Third World nations. In the summmer of 1989, Taiwan sent three quarters of a million dollars to San Francisco to aid the city's earthquake victims. Taiwan will likely continue to use its financial and economic resources to advance its international standing.

NOTES

1. The brief description of the historical origin of the opium wars is based on Jean Chesneaux, Marianne Bastid, and Marie-Claire Bergere, *China from the Opium Wars to the Nineteen Hundred Eleven Revolution* (New York: Pantheon, 1976).

2. For a detailed account of the modernization movements during the Ching Dynasty, see *China from the Opium Wars to the Nineteen Hundred Eleven Revolution*.

3. *The Political Doctrines of Sun Yat-Sen* by Paul Lineborger (Baltimore: Johns Hopkins University Press, 1937) carries a thorough introduction of the theory of livelihood.

5 GOVERNMENT AND TECHNOCRATS

The development of a national economy requires the allocation of resources and the regulation of economic activities. During economic development, the state, regardless of its form or ideology, must assume a major role, for it alone has the power and resources to execute the allocation and regulation. China's nationalistic approach to economic development and Dr. Sun Yat-Sen's designation of government responsibility in constructing its national economy predefined a strong leadership role for the Nationalist government. Taiwan's economists categorize the nation's economy as mixed: a combination of the planned and market economy. Only after 1985 did the government initiate a deliberate policy of noninterference in the economy. Over the last four decades the government's role in the economy has undergone a clear change in response to changing economic conditions and to the maturation of both the economic structure and the business enterpreneurs.

We will begin our discussion of the government's role in Taiwan's economy by first examining the prevailing governing philosophy of the Chinese state with respect to the economy. The Chinese believe the government has a twofold responsibility for the people's economic life—to ensure their basic economic welfare, and to administer economic justice through equal distribution of income. The government's responsibility for providing its people with the basic necessities is a concept as old as Chinese history itself. In imperial China, this responsibility was enforced by the mythical political belief that the emperor's absolute power and authority were conferred by a mandate of heaven. Thus, he was called the son of heaven and was charged with the sacred responsibility of looking after the welfare of his people. This heavenly mandate was good only as long as the emperor was capable of delivering the entrusted responsibility. As noted earlier, economic hardship, famine, and natural catastrophe were read as signs of heavenly withdrawal of the mandate and implied divine approval of overthrowing the throne.

In the absence of a democratic system to protect the interests of the weak, the powerless, and the poor, the religious element of the Chinese imperial power functioned through the conscience of the rulers and the collective sanctions of the people to ensure that the people's interests were heeded. When the Republic of China was founded in 1911, this govern-ment responsibility was written into the constitution. However, during the thirty-eight year history of the Nationalist government prior to its retreat to Taiwan, China fought a series of wars—against the warlords, the civil war, and the war against the Japanese. These wars consumed so much of the government's resources that the economic welfare of the Chinese people, especially the farmers and the urban factory workers, was woefully neglected. Over time, this negligence led to the massive defection of the farmers and factory workers to the Chinese Communists who advocated class struggle against the repressive landlords and urban capitalists. The strong grass-roots support for the Communists eventually led to the Nationalist downfall. The devastating defeat taught the Nationalists an important lesson: neither the Chinese ruling class, the elite, the middle class, or the intelligentsia alone could make the crucial judgment on the government's performance in serving its citizenry, and discontented masses could easily bring down a ruling power. Following its defeat and sub-sequent retreat, the Nationalist government corrected its intellectual- and middle-class-centered political view and began to attend to the needs of the lower classes.

During the government's early days on Taiwan, its survival was depend-ent on its ability to fix a collection of grave problems that threatened the economy—rampant inflation, mass unemployment, resettlement of a huge number of war refugees, and devastating postwar economic conditions. These challenges required the government to make a drastic policy switch from its traditional commitment to military economic reconstruction. The disintegrating economy was potentially as fatal as the military threat from the mainland.

Two major policy directions testified to the government's newly adopted political focus on the welfare of the masses. First, the government was as committed to stabilizing the economy as it was to promoting economic growth. By doing so, the government managed to avoid the nagging high inflation that often accompanies rapid economic growth and a widening gap between the country's rich and poor. This twin problem had unfailingly plagued Third World nations in the early stages of their economic development. Second, the government ensured equal economic opportunity to all regardless of economic status. In the 1950s it began promoting labor-intensive industries over technology-intensive industries which other Third World nations at a simlar developmental stage, such as Korea, had opted to favor. Labor-intensive industries were chosen because of their potential for creating jobs and easing unemployment problems.

The government's equal opportunity policy measures can be divided into four categories:

1. Making available to all people the resources required for entrepreneurial endeavors—capital, marketing and product information, and technical and management assistance.
2. Ensuring equal access to education.
3. Providing low-cost, high-quality training in specialized, advanced business and technical fields.
4. Making venture capital available to farmers and small business entrepreneurs.

In addition, land reform programs, government-sponsored technical assistance to agriculture, the farmers' association, and the farmers' credit union made farming a highly enterprising business in Taiwan. Government efforts to promote labor-intensive industries, along with its technical and management support of small- and medium-sized enterprises, helped to create, a new class of small- and medium-sized business entrepreneurs among factory workers. Thus, the two disadvantaged social groups, the farmers and factory workers, became active participants in their country's economy.

The government's planning role was originally forged to answer the special needs of Taiwan's economy at the time of the relocation. Taiwan's economy had been decimated by the war. Furthermore, the departure of the Japanese colonial government and businesses, left a structural and administrative void in the economy. Since the Japanese had systematically banned employment of Taiwanese for management positions, few Taiwanese were sufficiently competent to assume management responsibilities in business, industry, and government. In addition, Taiwan's economy was running at three-digit annual inflation rates, refugees from the mainland had exacerbated the already widespread postwar unemployment problem, and with refugees and relocated government employees and military personnel arriving daily, the population suddenly swelled by 20 percent. Clearly, the magnitude and urgency of Taiwan's economic problem demanded radical measures; organized initiatives needed to be introduced to speed up the restoration process. With the private sector too weak and fragmented to respond to the challenge, the government, which now controlled over 40 percent of all businesses, stepped in and assumed all responsibility for economic development projects.

The government did not have a written economic development plan in place until 1953. Even so, from 1949 to 1953, it launched a number of economic programs to progressively restore the economy.[1] Top priority was given to controlling inflation, rebuilding the infrastructures, and increasing agricultural and industrial production. To combat inflation, a series of monetary reforms were implemented, interest rates were raised to encourage savings, and prices were placed under strict control. Government engineers were commissioned to reconstruct damaged highways, airports, harbors, electrical power generation plants, and other facilities. In 1949 the first of a series of land reform programs was inaugurated—the farmland rent control policy to fix the ceiling of rent at 37.5 percent of total annual yields. With local government cooperation, the Nationalist government initiated a number of projects to improve agricultural technology, including constructing irrigation systems, developing better crops and livestock, and promoting the use of chemical fertilizers.

After 1953 nine consecutive economic development plans were implemented. Each plan identified specific development goals based on careful consideration of prevailing economic needs, available resources, and economic capability. The Council on Economic Development of the Executive Yuan and its predecessors were responsible for developing these plans. The Council usually gathered input from government offices in charge of agriculture, industry, energy resources, transportation, mine, military, finance, foreign trade, and education. The finished development plan was then distributed to the appropriate government office with specific implementation guidelines.

In addition to functioning as economic planner, the government actively facilitated economic growth through (1) controlling the interest rate, the foreign exchange rate, and the rate of import duties; (2) maneuvering the power and influence of government-owned enterprises, and the purchases and sales of government-owned lands; and (3) upgrading technical and management resources. For example, the government's success in the late 1950s in steering the economy from an import-substitution to an export-expansion orientation illustrates its apparent facilitator role in Taiwan's economy.

The government offered a number of new incentive measures to encourage export activities:

1. Customs duty rebates on defense surtax, and harbor tax and commodity tax rebates on materials imported for manufacturing products for export.
2. Exemptions from business and related stamp taxes.
3. A 2 percent deduction of total export earnings from taxable personal income.
4. A 10 percent income tax reduction for companies in manufacturing, mining, or handicrafts which, during the previous year, had exported 50 percent or more of their annual production outputs.
5. Provisions for retaining foreign exchange earnings, together with the privileges of selling foreign exchange permits for profits.
6. Special low interest loans to finance preshipment production and for raw materials purchases.
7. Government-guaranteed export insurances.

To boost Taiwan's export performance, the government encouraged the major export industries of the time—textile, canned mushrooms and asparagus spears, and citronella oil—to form trade associations so that production and pricing could be regulated through controlled export quotas and unified price quotations. As a result, some manufacturing associations, such as those for cotton spinning, steel and iron, rubber products, monosodium glutamate, woolen fabrics, and paper and paper products, subsidized their exported products. These subsidies actually amounted to private levies on their products sold on domestic markets. To further strengthen the competitiveness of export products, the government provided free services in export inspection, management, technical, and trade consultations, and market research, and assisted the participation of Taiwanese businesses in international trade shows and exhibits. The United Fund for Promotion and Expansion was established and financially supported by a mandatory contribution of 0.0625 percent of export earnings of the manufacturers. This has been the financial backing of the China External Trade Development Council, the government's powerful arm for promoting exports since its founding in 1970.

To remove obstacles to foreign investment (the obstacles usually coming from the bureaucratic complexity of acquiring industrial lands, obtaining permits for industrial construction, and applying for tax rebates by export-oriented businesses), the government built three tax and duty free export processing industrial zones. In each there is a government-funded administrative office staffed with personnel representing all government offices in charge of processing the application of business registrations, import and export licenses, and foreign exchange permits. Through the years, these industrial zones have attracted domestic and foreign investors alike, especially those in industries such as electronic products, garments, and plastic products.

The government also exhibited strong leadership in industry, especially in identifying and championing new development directions. Since Taiwan's young industry had limited resources and experience, the government assumed responsibility for industry services in research and development and technical training, which were prerequisite to introducing new technologies in industry. The successful transplantation of the advanced computer technology industry to Taiwan exemplified the government's facilitator role in introducing new technologies to industry. Like any other major government decision, the idea to transfer Western and Japanese computer technology first circulated among the core government officials for feedback; then it was discussed in the mass media to obtain public reactions; and finally, overseas experts, especially those of Chinese descent, were asked for their analyses and evaluations. Only then was the government ready to adopt the idea.

To assist the development and growth of high tech industries, the government built an approximately 35 square mile industrial park, fashioned after Silicon Valley in California, to house high tech companies. To fill the high tech research, development, and education function void in industry, the government founded the Industrial Technology Research Institute, the country's highest science and technology research organization, equipped it with state of the art research instruments, and staffed it with the best science and technical minds it could recruit. Taiwan's integrated circuit manufacturing technology was a hybrid product of a transferred technology from RCA and the institute's research efforts. In addition to the research and development function, the institute also offered consultation services and training programs to industry.

As is obvious from our discussion, the government had a heavy hand in the operation and growth of the economy. Taiwan's economic policies and related legislation were carefully designed, instituted in a timely fashion, and effectively implemented with respect to their designated missions. However, economic observers agreed that the high degree of cohesion within the government led to the unusually high level of coordination and efficiency in the legislation and policy implementation. This cohesion was also observed to be a result of the type of government leadership that operated on Taiwan and the deep loyalty of the government officials to their leaders.

Apparently, both the traditional political thought that grew out of China's feudalistic political structure and the Chinese nationalism that was the product of the modern Chinese experience with foreign aggression helped shape modern Taiwan's political leadership. The special sense of wartime urgency and the constant fear of invasion from the Chinese Communists helped to consolidate the people's support for strong government leadership. What is more, the presidencies of Chiang Kai-Shek and Chiang Chien-Kuo, which covered a span of thirty-six years, epitomized the government's strong leadership. Political scientists in Taiwan termed this leadership the "political leadership of a strongman." Under this kind of leadership, when a major issue came up, the president would seek opinions and suggestions from leading statesmen, work with his staff on the input, and then formulate his own decisions which would become the government's positions. Until recent years, the National Assembly and the Legislative Senate readily accommodated the chief of the state's views.

The strong leadership of the head of the state was primarily a product of the government officials and legislative bodies' deep reverence for and trust in their national leader. The strong leadership of the executive in Taiwan may also have been a natural response to the expectations of the traditional Chinese feudalistic mentality. All this is speculation; the important point is that the strong leadership might be responsible for the high degree of cohesion within the Nationalist government which allowed the government to effectively play the facilitator's role.

As the country's economy began to take off, a handful of government officials were charged with designing and engineering the economic development. Later, these officials held high positions in the government—vice president of the country, minister or deputy ministers of economic affairs or finance, or head of strategically important economic planning or development agencies. Among them were Chen Cheng, a vice president under Chiang Kai-Shek, who was responsible for the successful land reforms on the island; Chung-Yuang Yin, who engineered the early monetary and fiscal reforms; and Kwoh-Ting Li, whose long career with the government includes service as minister of economic affairs and of finance, and who engineered the development and growth of the country's high tech industry.

These and other leading government officials provided role models for a new class of young, aggressive, committed government officials who have now become the central force behind the gigantic forward movement of the economy. They are the so-called technocrats of the government; they are accomplished engineers, scientists, or economists, and through their government positions they introduced leading edge technologies or the lastest economic theories and applications. Therefore, they have enormous respect, authority, and power within the government. The majority of them are Western educated and have distinguished themselves by authoring popular economic policies, heading up successful major economic development projects, managing prominent economic development agencies, or accomplishing international trade negotiations. Certainly, the government's flexible structural environment facilitated their contributions. In fact, they were given ample latitude in defining their job responsibilities and in interpreting the scope of their positions. The loosely structured governmental process also spared these officials from bureaucratic obstacles that could otherwise prevent a speedy and effective implementation of policies or programs. It is evident that, within the Nationalist government, loyalty to the chief of the state and to the ruling party has been the prime criteria determining a person's selection to a prominent position. The majority of these technocrats either are the offspring of current or retired senior government officials or were selected and nurtured by the party early in their careers, some even while they were still in school. Accordingly, their loyalty to the leader and the party is unquestionably firm and solid. Their absolute loyalty added to government cohesion.

Probably because of scholar-official tradition in the Chinese government, a large proportion of government officials in Taiwan are learned professionals in their own specialized fields. High-ranking government officials are expected to be conversant in, and to keep abreast of, technical knowledge underlying major economic issues in Taiwan, whether the latest integrated circuit technology, the operational principles of the international monetary market, or U.S. foreign trade policy and legislation. In Taiwan high-ranking officials make competent use of technical jargon and technical theories in debates among themselves and in communications with the public. Since technical competency is a crucial criterion in determining their career success, many officials seek out highly trained consultants to serve on their staff or as their resource persons. Therefore, resourceful officials establish contacts with the world's most renowned scholars in order to obtain the latest and most authoritative information. Public expectations and competition among themselves motivate high-ranking government officials to remain highly knowledgeable and most current about major economic issues in Taiwan. Because of the extremely competitive environment in the government and the well-educated, watchful, and critical Taiwanese public, Taiwan's economic development policies and programs appear to have been well conceived and effectively implemented, and the government seems to be making informed economic decisions.

Clearly the technocrats in Taiwan's government have been making another type of contribution to the economy. That is, the example they have set as government officials has become a model for modern Chinese government employees—competency and high ethical standards. This official image is diametrically different from what the traditional Chinese mandarins projected. In the last twenty-one years, economic success has produced unprecedented affluence. While most people have experienced great improvement in their material well-being, government employees still draw unadjusted, stable salaries that are in no way comparable to compensations offered in the private sector. Their true job rewards have come from their ability to contribute and sometimes to obtain public recognition.

The government remains in close dialogue with the people on issues relating to economic policies and programs. Taiwan is a small island country with a closely knit population, and the government's apparatus extends to every level and corner. Therefore, it is not difficult to collect public opinions. In addition, as a gesture of openness, high-ranking government officials frequently visit businessmen, merchants, and entrepreneurs to get feedback on government policies and programs. When the government entertains a new economic policy or program, the mass media usually carry public debates on it. The public consensus that may emerge during these debates often becomes the guideline to finalizing the policy or program. Since an ill-conceived policy or program could cost the involved officials their jobs, officials are very cautious to feel the public pulse. Generally, the government responds quickly to business and industry needs. However, the officials, concerned with the public's evaluation of their performance, do not risk responding to problems whose successful outcomes are not publicly perceived. This reservation may explain the government's slowness to tackle deep, difficult problems.

Taiwanese business and industry customarily depend on government for guidance and assistance. Since the early 1950s, the government has shouldered responsibility for the growth of business and industry. Because of this early experience, Taiwan's business sector has grown dependent on the government to identify business growth directions, open up new international markets, develop international customers, and shield businesses from the impact of oil shortages or inflation. Therefore, it was not without reason that a large group of business representatives showed up at the front gate of the Ministry of Legislation building following the 1987 stock market crash to demand that the government reinstate an earlier market price. Taiwanese businesspeople believe that the government can and will do anything for the economy's well-being. However, as the dynamics of Taiwan's economy becomes more complex and business and industry grow more sophisticated, the extent to which the government can interfere in the economy is bound to be restricted and the impact of government assistance on the success of the island's businesses reduced. The time has probably come for Taiwanese businesses and industries to assume more responsibility for their own success, especially in the area of research and development and marketing.

The government's heavy involvement in Taiwan's economy raises doubts about the prospect for a free market economy on the island. With respect to this problem, three areas of government activities are of special concern: (1) the existence of a high proportion of government-owned businesses; (2) the government's strong hand in Taiwan's monetary market; and (3) the government's heavy protection of business and industry through import controls. Granted that past circumstances and conditions required a dominant government role, economists agree that the present economy can best benefit from free market functions. In 1987 the government declared that its major economic policy goal was to remove obstacles to the free operation of market forces.

On the issue of government-owned businesses, the proportion of government-owned businesses on the island dropped from 56.6 percent in 1952 to 10.2 percent in 1989. During the colonial period, the Japanese owned all major businesses. When Taiwan was retroceded to China in 1945, these businesses were handed over to the Nationalist government. It thus raised the number of government-owned businesses to a high proportion of the total number of businesses. In 1952 the government operated the entire public utility industry, and among the manufacturing and mining industry privately owned businesses accounted for only less than half the total number of businesses in these industries. Since then, with government-owned enterprises transferred to private ownership and the government's heavy investing in private enterprises, the proportion of government-owned businesses has thus been reduced. In 1959 the proportion of private enterprises exceeded that of government-owned businesses for the first time. In 1975 private businesses constituted 81.2 percent of total businesses. However, the worldwide economic stagnation after two oil crises depressed business investments in Taiwan, while the government, in an effort to boost the economy, invested heavily in new businesses especially in steel, copper, aluminum, shipbuilding, and the petrochemical industry. As a result, the proportion of government-owned enterprises once again rose. Nevertheless, private businesses continued to be the mainstream in Taiwan's economy. In 1989 private businesses accounted for 89.8 percent of the total number of businesses.

With regard to the government's control over Taiwan's monetary market, the central point of concern has been the government's control of interest rates. The government's apparatus for controlling the monetary market has been the Central Bank of Taiwan. The measures used by the Central Bank of Taiwan to fight the inflation caused by the oil crises of the 1970s were typical of the bank's control measures, namely (1) raising the prime interest rate, (2) issuing bank savings notes and certificates, (3) lifting restrictions on the amount of monies permitted to remit to foreign countries, (4) restricting the flow of money into Taiwan, and (5) increasing the supply of foreign exchange to importers. Most effective was raising the interest rates. For example, between July 1973 and January 1974, the prime interest rate was lifted three times, and the annual interest rate for one-year deposits increased from 8.75 to 15 percent. Higher interest rates indeed resulted in a marked growth in savings deposits—from 19 percent in 1973 to 37 percent in 1974. This was the exact response the government expected, that is, to absorb excessive money supplies. Soon after prices were stabilized, in June 1977 interest rates were cut, and the annual interest rate for savings deposits dropped to 9.5 percent.

In the meantime the government also lowered the prime lending rate in order to sustain economic growth. Beginning in 1980, it started to loosen its control over interest rates, and guidelines for bank interest rates, which would allow the interest rate to reflect the real situation in the money supply market, were legislated. To prepare the way for a free monetary market, the government asked the banks to devise universally acceptable tactics for determining prime bank lending rates. In 1985 ten major banks together with the Bank of Small- and Medium-Sized Businesses, the Farmers' Bank, and the Fisherman's Bank, all supported the unified prime lending rate. In the same year, all government regulations on bank interests were abolished. To increase the international banking and financial institutes' accessibility to Taiwan's monetary market, in 1984 the government announced detailed guidelines for international monetary transfers. To date, fifteen banks in Taiwan have received permits to open up branch offices to handle international banking transactions. Since 1986 foreign banks have been allowed to set up branches in Taiwan, and restrictions previously placed on the scope of their business operations have been relaxed.

During the early years of the Nationalist government in Taiwan, customs duties were used to protect the country's then nascent industry. However, economic policies were quite successful in expanding international trade as well as strengthening the international competitiveness of Taiwan's products. Soon Taiwan started to accumulate trade surpluses. At this point, the government recognized the need to avoid any international frictions that could result from unbalanced trade with other nations as well as the need for Taiwanese products to have access to international markets. Therefore, in 1983 the government began liberalizing its customs system and increasing the openness of its market to foreign goods. For example, in 1986 the two highest duty categories in Taiwan's customs system were lowered to 31.77 percent and 22.83 percent, respectively, from an average of 48 percent in 1978 and an average of 30 percent in 1983.

It is difficult, if not impossible, to prescribe an ideal model of government policies and measures for the development of a Third World national economy. Provided that such models could be found, they might not even carry much practical value in real situations. Nonetheless, some general statements can be made about the Nationalist government's success in developing Taiwan's economy. In retrospect, we can see that the government had no choice but to assume the awesome challenge of rapidly developing the island's economy. The government's relocation to Taiwan afforded it the unprecedented opportunity to rid itself of cultural, social, and institutional baggage that it had fought so hard to shed during its earlier modernization efforts on the mainland. In addition, the more modern and manageable social and economic conditions on the island might have contributed to its economic success.

The Nationalist government's lack of experience in economic development was compensated by its search for and application of the latest theories and technologies. Its most important economic measures were those that recognized the needs of the people and that promoted equal income distribution. Some observers believe that the open and practical mindedness of the government officials resulted in timely, practical economic policies in Taiwan. When judged against the Western standard of democracy, the Nationalist government might not represent the most perfect democratic form in the world, but their newfound affluence and prosperity have given the Taiwanese a deep interest in working together to achieve peaceful political reforms. With the coming of age of Taiwan's business, industry, and financial and monetary institutions, and the government's commitment to a free market economy, less government domination of the economy is in the offing.

NOTE

1. Executive Yuan, Council on Economic Development, *The Journey of the Modernization of Taiwan's Economy* (Taipei: Bureau of Economic Research, 1987), p. 14.

6   ECONOMIC POLICIES

Economic policies are designed to set into motion certain institutional and market dynamics to produce desired results. This chapter examines economic policies in Taiwan to reveal how policy stimuli were used to guide the economy toward desired economic development and growth. Tracing the interplay between the major economic policies and the growth that occurred in the economy will reveal the underlying causal relations between policies and programmed changes. The findings might be of interest to those who look for applicable lessons in Taiwan's economic development experience. For this reason and others, Taiwan's economic policies stand out as a colorful and dynamic component of the development history of its economy.

Dr. Sun Yat-Sen's economic ideology had a predominant influence on shaping Taiwan's economic policies. The following five concepts which Dr. Sun described were the most influential: (1) equal sharing among the people of the fruits of the economy, (2) private ownership of business and property, (3) preservation of the market functions, (4) institution of checking measures to prevent corporate monopoly of the basic life-sustaining materials and services, and (5) the government's responsibility to build infrastructures to enable continuing economic growth.

The government made a firm commitment to the economic interest of the working people while not stifling profitmaking incentives. In the 1950s the series of land reform laws and the policy for promoting agriculture production were designed to raise the income level of the agricultural sector, thereby correcting an unfair tradition in the Chinese economy: that is, the Chinese farmers had always been at the bottom of the economic structure. In the late 1950s the increased agricultural production began to yield surpluses that were used to subsidize industry. In turn, the farmers' improved economic condition made them a resourceful purchasing power in the marektplace, which helped sustain the newly established industrial sector of the economy. Later in the 1960s the government's policy to expand international trade included a strategical plan to develop the labor-intensive industries. The option to develop these industries was chosen because of the government's commitment to ease the unemployment problem. This policy choice proved to be prudent, for within seven years not only was the widespread unemployment problem cured, but also the labor market actually began to experience labor shortages.

Taiwan's international trade brought stability and wealth to the nation's business and industry. In the early 1980s the government realized that business and industry were now ready to support legislation that extended protection to the workers in the workplace. In 1983 a comprehensive labor law, modeled after similar laws in developed countries, was passed in Taiwan. A milestone had thus been reached in ensuring the welfare of working men and women.

During the last few years, the skyrocketing appreciation of Taiwan dollars and the new international trade policy measures adopted by the Nationalist government under U.S. pressure for balanced trade brought hardships to Taiwan's business and industry. Most hard hit were the farmers and small business owners. The government set about to help them develop strategies to offset these negative developments. The government also launched a number of countermeasures, including encouraging the domestic consumption of agricultural products, assisting manufacturing automation in production plants to help industry regain international competitiveness, and developing new world markets for Taiwanese products, such as those markets in Eastern Europe and Russia with which trade had previously been prohibited for political reasons.

The Nationalist government's leadership role in the economy has been less visible in recent years. The policy theme that underlies the current stage is clearly depoliticization. The government, as well as business and industry, recently reached agreement following a long dialogue that the island's economy had matured to a point that it could benefit most from the free, unimpeded operation of the market.

Kwoh-Ting Li, in *The Evolution of Policy Behind Taiwan's Development Success*, demonstrates that a clear evolutionary process underlies the development of the country's economic policies—from the early days when the government had a heavy hand in the economy to the later gradual withdrawal of government interference, and finally, to the present return of the economy to the control of market functions. He calls the journey of the island's economy "a liberalization process," and he identifies ten policy areas that have undergone this process: taxation, customs duties, interest rates, foreign exchange rates, foreign capital, government-owned enterprises, agricultural policy, manpower and labor policy, science and technology, and economic development plans. Taiwanese government officials echoed Li's prediction in the book that Taiwan's future economic policies will continue a course of depoliticizing and liberalizing the economy and moving toward its total integration into the world's economic structure.

Taiwan's economic policies embodied a number of distinctive development strategies. First, the government emphasized the importance of an economic environment capable of stimulating and nurturing the individual's natural ability to carry out his or her profitmaking activities. It counted on the ripple effects created by these activities to lead the economy to self-propelled growth. For instance, the primary goal of the country's land reform policy in the late 1940s and early 1950s was to give the farmers needed production incentives—full ownership of their land and the sole benefits from their labor. Thus, the land reform policy removed the major obstacle to enterprising farming. To further assist the farmers in turning farming into business enterprise, the government disseminated new agricultural technologies to farms, made available agricultural loans, and upgraded rural infrastructures. As the agricultural economy grew and expanded, the government even helped find international markets for the agricultural products. Through the years, the government's guidance enabled the farmers to develop their own business acumen and marketing abilities in agricultural exports.

The successful growth of the agricultural economy not only satisfied domestic demand for agricultural products, but also generated enough capital to subsidize Taiwan's early industrial development. Then, in the late 1950s similar tactics were used again to encourage the growth of the island's young industry. These tactics were embodied in the following policies: low interest industrial loans, government-funded technical supports, government-guaranteed purchases of industrial output, transfers of successful government enterprises to private ownership, favorable foreign exchange rates for industrial equipment and materials acquisitions, and protected domestic markets. It was during this period that the business empire of many of today's Taiwanese industrial magnates began, such as Yuan-Ching Wang, a giant in Asia's petrochemical industry.

A second development strategy embodied a pragmatic approach to the development sequence. The five stages identified in the developmental course of Taiwan's economy are, in order: (1) the modernization of the agriculture, (2) the import substitution orientation of the industry, (3) economic growth through export expansion, (4) the development of heavy and petrochemical industries, and (5) the promotion of high tech industries. The development goal and orientation of each stage were carefully selected, based on analysis of economic needs and evaluation of resources then available. Entering each new economic development stage was more the natural result of steering the economic forces already in progress to a desired economic orientation than a newly fabricated economic condition that had no connection with the previous state of the economy.

The obvious absence of a political ideology in selecting the economic development course in Taiwan is extraordinary for a Third World economy. The government's pragmatic approach to economic development facilitated the later decision of depoliticization. Granted that the government at the beginning of each new economic development stage needed to facilitate its transition to a new development stage, as soon as the dynamics of the economy were aligned with the targeted economic development orientation, the economy was left to operate on its own with no further external interference. Thus, policy interferences with the economy were confined to the initial period of each development stage. When economic policies were applied only to facilitate the transition to new economic development orientations as was the case in Taiwan the desired economic growth would be possible and would thus make the economy's continuous depedency on government interference unnecessary.

There have been exceptions in the case of Taiwan's economic policies. The policy to promote the development of Taiwan's automobile industry is a case in point. The government made a major commitment to establish an automobile industry when the nation's general industrial capability was still too young for such an ambitious endeavor. Therefore, even though for thirty years government policies had granted the highest tax deduction privilege in Taiwan's tax history to the industry, protected the industry's domestic market from foreign competition, and supported the industry with government-guaranteed purchases, the automobile industry did not take off as the government had intended. The automobile industry's experience is a classical example of how long-term reliance on privileges and government protection retarded the industry's ability to develop the product competitiveness required to venture into the international market.

The third development strategy has to do with Taiwan's evolution toward an open economy. Being an island economy with limited natural resources, Taiwan depends heavily on international trade for materials as well as hard currencies. Even though in the early years import customs duties and foreign exchange rates were used lavishly to discourage imports in order to protect the island's nascent industry, the government instituted policies to guarantee favorable rates on customs duties and foreign exchange for importing industrial materials and equipment. In the late 1950s as the markets became flooded with the products of the industries initially set up only to achieve a modest goal of substituting the island's imports, the government immediately took a diametrical shift to promote exports. Thus, the policies established earlier to enforce a multiple foreign exchange rate to favor Taiwan's import-substituting industries were quickly abolished. The new orientation of the 1960s to expand Taiwan's exports necessitated that the government open up Taiwan's own market to foreign goods in order to maintain its privileged status with its major trading partners. Subsequently, the government adopted policies to ease import restrictions and other trade barriers. However, significant improvements in this area came only in recent years when the government took giant steps to reduce customs duties and to relax other import controls. Of course, as a step toward creating an open economy, no measures were bolder than the government's recent efforts to integrate Taiwan's monetary market, banking, and insurance industry into the world's financial system.

Finally, the government's ability to keep its policymaking process free from the influence of interest groups in effect eliminated a major source of political interference to the economy. Apparently, the economic policies instituted in Taiwan had been intended solely for the island's overall economic welfare. The absence of political pressure on policymaking may be explained by the following reasons. The government's relocation to Taiwan serendipitously ended the long tradition of government officials linking closely with local powers. The high professional standards set by the technocrats in the government made it difficult for interest groups to establish private connections with the government through which to exert any influence over government decisions. In addition, the government's ingrained commitment to an equalized distribution of income produced a politically harmonious society in Taiwan in which no group's right to economic justice had been violated or neglected. Therefore, the government had no prevailing need to apply force to correct any situation that might threaten economic justice as has often been done in Third World countries.

Since 1949, the Nationalist government has manipulated bank interest, foreign exchange, and taxes to effect desired changes in the economy. For instance, when high inflation threatened the nation's economic stability, high interest rates were instituted to encourage savings. On the other hand, when investments in the economy showed signs of slowing down, interest rates were lowered to attract business borrowings. Again, a system of multiple foreign exchange rates with separate rates for importers and exporters and for importing different categories of items were instituted to afford privileged rates to importers of industrial materials and equipment. The expectation was that these privileged treatments would lower the manufacturing costs of Taiwan's industrial products. Low manufacturing costs were expected to boost the products' competitiveness in the international markets. In turn, a good export performance was expected to draw further investments into the island's industry. In addition, from time to time corporate tax holidays were offered as an incentive to encourage the establishment of new industries, especially high tech industries. Business and industry responded well to all forms of tax incentives.

The government's success in applying policies to produce desired changes in the economy had a great deal to do with the fact that these policies had been carefully designed to be in congruence with the culture and traditions of the people. The government's determination to reserve a place for agriculture in the economy is a case in point. The government's decision to run a dual economy—to allow both agriculture and industry to grow and expand side by side—indicates its determination to preserve agriculture as a permanent element in Taiwan's economy. Since abundant harvests from the land symbolize prosperity to the Chinese, in order to sustain the public's confidence in the economy it is paramount that the government keep the country agriculturally self-sufficient.

Taiwan's economic policies also paid special attention to the place of the family in Chinese life. In traditional Chinese society, the high degree of solidarity and corporation among family members made the family a natural production unit in the economy. This tradition, of course, was more pronounced in the agricultural than in the industrial sector. Land reform programs and policies for assisting small- and medium-sized enterprises indicate the government's desire to encourage the production modes that capitalize family as a production unit. Under the land reform programs, a Taiwanese farmer was guaranteed an opportunity to purchase a certain size of farmland, depending on the grade of the land, which was considered to be the most appropriate size for the average farming family working together as a production unit. Later, the growth and development of Taiwan's labor-intensive industries spawned a large number of family-owned small- and medium-sized manufacturers. Since then this type of enterprise has been the predominant size and form of business in Taiwan. In fact, the flexibility and adaptability unique to these businesses permitted the economy's extraordinary adjustability to difficult international challenges.

Among the policy measures designed to assist small- and medium-sized businesses were the founding of the Bank of Small- and Medium-Sized Businesses, government-sponsored sales and marketing organizations to help bring the products of these businesses to international markets, government-funded trade and exhibit centers to introduce the products of these businesses to international buyers, and government-organized overseas business trips to expose these businesses to foreign markets. The addition of the Small- and Medium-Sized Business Administration to the administrative structure of the Ministry of Economic Affairs clearly illustrates the government's strong support to small- and medium-sized business.

The government warmly invited overseas Chinese to participate in the island's major political decisions and events. The government valued the support of the overseas Chinese and generously invested in programs that courted their continuous support. Policies formulated to attract their investment in the economy included handsome corporate tax deductions and low interest loans to business ventures. Not surprisingly, after the United States cut off economic aid to Taiwan in 1965, overseas Chinese investments made up the largest part of the capital that replaced U.S. economic aid. Again, in the 1980s, the capital and technology brought in by the overseas Chinese were significant to the development of Taiwan's high tech industries.

The government also avoided applying any economic policies that might require sacrificing the island's political stability and harmony. Whenever cases arose where effecting changes in the economy would upset the nation's social or political harmony, creative policy measures were introduced to achieve desired changes without harmful social consequences. For instance, in the late 1940s and early 1950s, as a land reform measure, nonfarming landowners were required to sell their lands to landless farmers. Because of the traditional connotations of land for the Chinese, farmers had little hope of ever owning the land they tilled. The result was the notorious landlord institution in agriculture whereby the landlords would lease land to landless farmers to till. Often, the land rentals became the landlords' major income. Therefore, the landlords traditionally set land rentals so high that after collection the tenant farmers were left with little to feed their family. As a result, the farmers had no motivation to improve production.

An agriculture based on this kind of landownership and production system obviously has little chance for substantial growth. When the Nationalist government relocated to Taiwan, an area of about 871,000 hectares of cultivatable land, the government was expected to feed not hundred thousand government employees and their families. Under these circumstances, raising agricultural production immediately became an urgent task. The government launched its islandwide land reform programs even before beginning to implement those policy measures specifically designed to raise agricultural production such as improving farming technology, introducing new crops, and increasing the use of chemical fertilizers. Because of the emotions as well as the high monetary values attached to land owning, redistributing farmlands was the most difficult aspect of the land reform programs.

The government's demonstrated ability to accomplish this task expeditiously and, most importantly, peacefully, earned it much deserved acclaim. Several innovative policy measures were responsible for this success. First, the government instituted regulations on farmland rentals to fix the rent at 37.5 percent of total annual yields and to stipulate a legal binding power to land rental contracts to protect the tenant farmers' interests. As expected, this measure quickly reduced land values. Thus, when the government was ready to implement land redistribution, offering to buy lands from nonfarming landowners, the owners were more than willing to sell. Then, to channel the landowners' large capital gains from the sales transactions back into the economy and to encourage their investment in industry, the government paid the landowners partly in stocks of successful government-owned companies that were soon to be transferred to private ownership. Thus, those who had owned large tracts of lands now became the major stockholders of the island's industries. The Yuan-Ching Wang and Chen-Fu Koo empires began under such an arrangement.

The negative side of these successful economic policies was that charismatic leadership rather than an elaborate bureaucratic process now shaped these policies. As noted earlier, all of Taiwan's major economic policies since 1949 have been authored and supervised by prominent government officials. Since these policy proposals were endorsed by distinguished government officials and already had strong public support, the Ministry of Legislation would automatically approve them. In every case the author of the policy became de facto chief administrator of the implementation of the policy. Thus, the policies, though closely researched, could forego the usual deliberation and reviewing process that characterizes a multilevel government bureaucratic system. As a result, the sponsoring officials of the policies often failed to foresee their total impact on society and had little opportunity beforehand to organize the support of other government agencies. Consequently, the government often learned about the negative impacts of the policies through angry public reaction. In addition, only through a dissatisfied public did the government recognize the need to coordinate the efforts of other government departments and agencies in the policy implementation. These shortcomings demonstrate the need for comprehensive policy planning and evaluation in the government as well as for increased use of social science tools.

Another problem area involves the lack of a formal policymaking body and process in Taiwan. When economic problems become too complex and politically risky for officials to offer policy solutions, the officials would wisely keep silent and the government was left with no direction. As a result, the public was left to deal with problems with no government assistance. A case in point is the excessive cash flow that occurred in the aftermath of the currency appreciation. Uncertain over the U.S. demand for a balanced trade with Taiwan and about the prospect of a deteriorating trade relationship with the United States, the Taiwanese lost interest in long-term investments. Consequently, Taiwanese of all social levels went on a gambling binge; the amount of monies gambled was astronomical, and the number of people who participated was overwhelming.

This same public frenzy was also responsible for sudden, large movements of capital into the young stock market. The huge amount of capital that flooded the market and the large volume traded daily transformed the market into a gigantic gambling place where ordinary people made millions of dollars overnight. The wild activity on the market not only upset the normal function of the economy, but also caused an unprecedented labor shortage. Because the market had become a profitable gambling center, many people quit their jobs, causing an acute labor shortage. While market prices kept adjusting to the rising value of the local currency, those who kept their jobs and drew incomes from steady salaries were severely hurt by the turbulent price rising. To keep pace with the wild price rises, these people brought their savings into the stock market. The government watched helplessly as this madness continued, convinced that the economy would eventually absorb the overflow capital and return to normal. Of course, the validity of this idea still awaits to be proved.

7 INDUSTRIALIZATION

For developing countries, industrialization is one of the few roads to rapid and steady economic growth. In the early 1960s industrialization allowed Taiwan to replace its agricultural export tradition with a new line of industrial exports—inexpensive manufacturing goods—to developed countries. This development spearheaded a phenomenal economic growth. When we examine Taiwan's industrialization experience, three questions immediately come to mind. First, with its poor resources, war-damaged infrastructure, serious postwar inflation, severe trade deficits, and shortages of foreign exchange, how did Taiwan achieve successful industrialization? Second, how did the country escape the grim fate that the dependency theorists had so surely predicted for export-oriented developing countries like Taiwan? They predicted that industrialization in these countries would unavoidably fall under the control of the industries in the advanced nations, and so these developing nations were doomed to become dependents of the industrial nations.[1] Third, how did the industrial sector achieve technological progress so speedily, progress that had taken Japanese industry much longer to reach? This chapter addresses each of these questions.

During their fifty-year colonial rule of Taiwan, the Japanese invested heavily in the economy. At least in five areas their legacy became the foundation of Taiwan's industrialization. First, rice and sugarcane were developed as export crops. The earnings from these two exports actually helped finance the island's early industrialization efforts. The colonial Japanese began developing the rice and sugar production immediately after they annexed the island. The Japanese need to develop the sugar industry was urgent inasmuch as their annual imports of sugar then exceeded 10 percent of its total import bill.[2] Enticed by various measures offered by the colonial government, the planting of sugarcane spread from the southern part of Taiwan to its colder north and mountainous east. Sugar mills, which could be owned only by the Japanese, mushroomed to the point that the colonial government had to regulate new establishments. After 1929, Taiwan was able to supply most of Japan's sugar demand. At its peak of production, in 1938–39, Taiwan produced 1.37 million metric tons of sugar, second only to Cuba among the world sugar producers.[3]

By 1900, when Japan began to experience rice shortages, rice imports from Taiwan made up the supply deficiency. However, in 1918, a severe rice shortage in Japan caused serious social problems, and the ruling party in Japan sought to increase the production of Pon Lai rice, the kind of rice the Japanese preferred. Beginning in 1920, experiments with planting Pon Lai rice took place in Taiwan. A decade of efforts brought a marked increase in both Taiwan's rice production and its rice exports to Japan.

When the Nationalist government took over in 1949, it wisely decided to continue the island's tradition of growing and exporting rice and sugar. Later, the land reforms, together with the introduction of technological improvements in agriculture, greatly increased agricultural output, including rice and sugar. For years thereafter rice and sugar remained Taiwan's major exports, and the earnings from agricultural exports supported the initial stage of industrialization. During the import substitution period of industrialization, the well-to-do agricultural sector's purchasing power helped sustain many of the island's nascent industries. Later, in 1960, as Taiwan embarked on a new stage of export-oriented industrialization with emphasis on expanding labor-intensive industries, the already higher agricultural productivity made it possible to release the surplus farm labor to the industries.

Second, the public utilities and communication facilities which the colonial Japanese built provided basic infrastructures for the Nationalist government's industrialization efforts. During the colonial period, the south-north railroad and the modern ports at Keelung and Kaohsiung were built to transport sugarcane harvested across the island to sugar mills for processing, and to ship rice and processed sugar to Japan. The construction of the hydroelectric power generating plant at Sun-Moon Lake was completed in 1934, which made low-cost electric power available. Irrigation facilities were widespread; the huge reservoir in the south was constructed between 1920 and 1930.[4] These facilities allowed the Nationalist government to quickly launch its industrialization efforts.

Third, industries established during the colonial period such as food processing, metallurgical, and chemical industries, later became the industrial foundations for Taiwan's industrialization. From 1900 to the mid-1930s, Taiwan exported agricultural products to Japan and in return imported manufactured goods from that country. During this period, Taiwan's industrial production was limited to agricultural products, chiefly sugar and rice, as well as some related products, such as sugar processing machinery, simple agricultural supplements, and tin cans for pineapple exports.[5] Later, with the expansion of Japanese influence in the East and in Southeast Asia, Taiwan's geographical proximity to Southeast Asia and south China made the island an ideal location, within the Japanese economic Empire, for processing certain raw materials brought in from these regions.

With its new role in the expanded Japanese economic sphere, Taiwan's industrial development took a new turn. Aside from processing industrial raw materials from agricultural products (the production of dehydrated alcohol from sugar molasses and sweet potatoes to provide a fuel alternative, tapioca, and various essences such as castor oil, and citronella oil for export to Japan and bagasse pulp for papermaking), Taiwan began to develop its metallurgical and chemical industries. These industries used raw materials such as salt, sulfur, and bagasse produced locally, silicon brought in from Manchuria, and bauxite from Southeast Asia to make products such as magnesium, ferroalloy, and aluminum which were shipped to Japan to support its wartime defense industry. Some of these products, however, such as pulp and paper and ammonium sulfate were oriented toward the local market. When the Chinese Nationalist government launched its first attempt at industrialization, such already established industries were targeted for expansion. Thus, supply sources in Southeast Asia were kept up and the Japanese market was reopened. In fact, the expansion of these industries permitted the subsequent development of the country's import substitution industries.

Fourth, the colonial Japanese completed and documented Taiwan's first comprehensive farmland survey and household registration. To facilitate the colonial government's policing function and tax collection, households were registered. Furthermore, in order to recover unaccounted tax revenues and to levy land taxes based on the size and grade of the land owned, a thorough land survey was performed throughout the island. These programs produced the first clear account of Taiwan's population and land survey which had conveniently readied the island for the later Nationalist government's land reform programs.

Finally, during the colonial period, new institutions and new behavioral patterns were established among the island's Chinese. These institutions and behavioral patterns had far-reaching effects on Taiwan's postwar economic development. Contemporary Taiwanese agricultural economists fondly point out the contributions of the farmers' association, an institution introduced by the colonial Japanese, to the area's agriculture.[6] The association was a self-help organization, and one of its major functions was to conduct experiments with new farming technologies and to help disseminate them to all farmers. This function greatly increased the farmers' power to control the physical and biological environment of farming and thus to raise their production. As noted earlier, agriculture's success contributed to industrialization's success.

The characteristic aggressiveness of today's Taiwanese trading firms had its roots in the business examples set by the colonial Japanese trading firms. The Japanese colonial government set up attractive inducements to encourage Japanese investment and trade in Taiwan. Partly because of the colonial law that prohibited full Taiwanese ownership of any stock companies during 1908–23, most industrial and trading activities were in Japanese hands.[7] For instance, the oligarchical Mitsui gained control of the total rice trade in Taiwan. After the Japanese repatriation, the Taiwanese began to fill the trade vacuum. The Taiwanese trading firms established during this time were modeled after the colonial Japanese trading firms in business operation and market competition. The aggressive, competitive trading firms of today are clearly the descendants of the colonial Japanese trading firms. In addition, the long Japanese colonial rule inevitably altered some of the traditional behavior patterns, especially the abandonment of the feudalistic mentality and the acquisition of an absorption capacity for industrial technology and modern ways of life.

Taiwan's colonial history left the island with an economical structure heavily rooted in agriculture. At the time of the retrocession, agricultural exports constituted 95 percent of total export income.[8] Reconstructing an economy from an agricultural- to an industrial-based one is a grave challenge to developing countries. The Taiwanese were able to do so through a commonly employed transformation strategy that was bidirectional in approach: (1) to increase investments in industry to improve its productivity and to enhance its diversity; and (2) to raise agricultural productivity to rapidly increase total agricultural output so that the agricultural sector could supply industrial materials and investment capital. With industrialization under way, the agricultural sector, with its purchasing power, could also support industry growth.

Taiwan chose first to develop its agriculture-related industries—sugar processing, canned foods, paper, tobacco and wine, castor oil, and citronella oil. As the economic development progressed, building materials industries such as cement, brick, glass, steel, and wood, energy resources such as petroleum products and electric power, and consumer industries such as foods, textile, soap, cleaning products, and home appliances all gradually developed. Among these industries, the production of textile, cement, glass, monosodium glumate, plywood, and plastic products quickly exceeded the demands of the domestic market and made way into the international markets. Because the industrial sector rapidly accumulated capital and made technological advancements during the initial stage of industrialization, industry progressed to a higher technology level. For example, the textile, plywood, plastic products, and electronic products industries made marked improvements in product quality, and they started to import higher grades of processing materials for production.

As more new industries were introduced, a better developed forward and backward supplier chain relationship emerged among the industries. In the meantime, in the agricultural sector, land reform programs, the introduction of advanced farming technology to the farmers, and the widespread rural development projects had all contributed to a significantly increased agricultural production in Taiwan—an average increase of 3.4 percent annually. The increased agricultural production was not a result of an increased acreage of arable land; instead, it was achieved through improved productivity on existing farmland. Therefore, the increased agricultural productivity created surplus farm labor. In the 1960s the government began to promote labor-intensive industries to absorb the surplus labor as well as to expand exports. This policy change resulted in an impressive 16.5 percent average annual industrial growth in the 1960s.

Taiwanese economists describe the course of industrialization on Taiwan as a five-stage process: (1) initial reconstruction (1945–49), (2) import substitution (1950–59), (3) export expansion (1960–69), (4) heavy and chemical industries (1970–79), and (5) strategic industries (1980–present). Each stage was distinguished by the types of industries developed during that period of time.

The initial reconstruction stage began immediately following retrocession. Industrial development during the prewar Japanese colonial period had centered on the agricultural product processing and consumer industries. During the war, the changing needs of the Japanese defense industry required the development of heavy industries such as steel, machinery, alumina processing, oil refinery, and shipbuilding on Taiwan. The war disrupted the implementation of many Japanese plans for developing Taiwan's industry. With regard to those already in operation, many industrial plants were either completely destroyed or were damaged extensively in the Allied bombing. Those few that survived suffered from lack of adequate maintenance during the war and a shortage of materials and operating personnel after the war. At retrocession, industrial production barely reached one-third of the highest production record set during the colonial period. After the war, the Nationalist government first restored the industrial plants and then carried out the unfinished industrial development plan drawn by the colonial Japanese.

The reconstruction efforts were slowed down by the postwar scarcity of competent personnel, materials, and capital. Only in 1950, after the United States resumed economic aid to Taiwan, did this task pick up speed. Constrained by the limited resources then available, the government initially concentrated on three types of industry: the electrical power generation industry, the industry that produced the main source of energy; the fertilizer industry, the industry on which the island's agriculture depended; and the textile industry, the island's basic consumer industry.[9] At the time, imports of fertilizers and textiles accounted for a significant portion of Taiwan's scarce foreign exchange.

Postwar restoration took three years. In 1942 the government started to implement economic development plans that were aimed primarily at allocating resources to facilitate economic growth. At this time, the island had not yet recovered from the rampant inflation which, according to many observers, was the immediate reason why the Nationalist government lost the mainland to the Chinese Communists. The government saw that only a sufficient supply of goods in the market would ease the inflation pressure on the economy. With the influx of mainlander refugees, Taiwan experienced a serious unemployment problem. At the same time, the government was running severe trade deficits and foreign exchange shortages. Facing these serious problems, the government made labor-intensive industries the focus of its first four-year development plan, based on the rationale that these industries required low capital investments, low level of technology, and a short period of time to complete production plant construction. These requirements fit well with Taiwan's existing economic capability.

The goal of the first four-year plan was to produce goods to replace major import items, and to increase production in order to meet market demands and alleviate the unemployment problem, inflation, and trade deficits. The second four-year plan essentially continued the program of the previous plan, although, for the first time, industries targeted for development now included some nonconsumer industries. The implementation of these two development plans helped develop a number of industries, including textile, foods, plywood, cement, glass, monosodium glutamate, chemical products, and electrical appliances. The market was soon flooded with their products, as a result of which these industries started to push their products into export markets. The industrial growth rate during these two periods was an annual average of 11.9 percent, a figure much higher than the records set for other developing economies of that era.

The first two economic plans coincided with the import substitution period of industrialization. The government's industry protection policies allowed the young industries to grow and gain control of the market which had previously been occupied by imported products. Prior to the import substitution stage of Taiwan's industry, imports had supplied more than 70 percent of total consumption. The government's industry protection measures consisted, on the one hand, of tighter restrictions on import quotas and higher foreign exchange rates to importers, and on the other hand, of favorable foreign exchange rates for importing industrial materials and equipment to help reduce domestic production costs.

Taiwan's import substitution industries grew and prospered under the government's policies. The import substitution industries were so sucessful that the market was saturated with their products, goods were sold at production costs, and plants operated at a level far below capacity. The fast growth of the import substitution industries rushed industrialization to its next stage, the export expansion period.[10]

In examining export prospects, Taiwan's economists realized that government protection had unexpectedly stifled industry's ability to compete in the open market and that to become competitive in the international market both production technology and costs needed to be improved substantially. The government's solution to the challenge was to upgrade the industry through increased industrial investments and, in the meantime, expand the export markets. Therefore, in 1958, trade and foreign exchange reforms were instituted to reset the emphasis of the nation's trades from import restriction to export expansion.

At the end of 1959, the government promulgated the famous nineteen point Program of Fiscal and Economic Reform. The purpose of the reform was to remove any obstacles which tax, import duty, or foreign exchange systems may have posed for the nation's industrialization progress. In 1960 the government set a new policy to encourage investments in business. The policy was designed to induce savings, investments, and export expansion through tax exemptions and reductions. It also provided for government assistance in procuring industrial land. The combined effects of these policies produced beneficial results in improved technology and productivity of those light industries that prospered during the earlier industrialization stage. The abundance of inexpensive and quality labor gave industries such as textile, plastic products, plywood, and electronic product assembly a strong competitive edge that earned them secured market shares in the world market. During this period, growth also took place in industries that employed higher technologies and demanded larger capital investments such as synthetic fiber, plastic materials, steel, machinery, automobile, and shipbuilding. The average annual industrial growth in the 1960s was at a record-setting rate of 16.5 percent.

In the late 1960s industry's growth generated a steady and sizable demand for industrial materials and product components. Since the stability and growth of most industries depended on the international pricing and supply of needed industrial materials and product components, and the industrial sector already had the capability to produce the materials and components industry needed, the government in the 1970s started to promote the development of heavy and chemical industries. It was hoped that these industries would assume responsibility for supplying the island's need for industrial intermediaries. This move inaugurated a new stage of industrialization: the development of heavy and chemical industries. The material industries such as steel, copper, and aluminum, transportation industries such as shipbuilding, automobile, and motorcycle, the petrochemical industries, and the machinery, motor, and electronic components industry had all experienced high growth in the 1970s.

The oil crises of the 1970s forced the highly energy-dependency industries such as steel, copper, and aluminum to scale down their production to a level that would just meet domestic demand. Rising oil prices and uncertain oil supplies prompted the government to concentrate on those industries that had a relatively low level of energy dependency, yet a high technology component, such as machinery, motor, electronic components, and fine instruments. These industries were targeted to produce goods capable not only of substituting Taiwan's imports but also of competing on the international market. The oil shortage of 1974 severely affected the economy in Taiwan, reducing its annual economic growth rate to a record-low 1.1 percent.

To restore the economy, the government launched ten massive public construction projects.[11] Between 1975 and 1977 this effort produced the highest economic growth record in Taiwan's history—an average annual rate of 13.9 percent and an average annual industrial growth rate of 22.5 percent. However, the worldwide recession and inflation triggered by the 1979 oil crisis sharply reduced the international demand for Taiwan's products, and in the meantime a resurgence of international protectionism threatened the growth of exports. High oil prices drove up the cost of Taiwan's products, causing them to lose their competitive edge in the world markets. Both the 1980s economic growth rate—6.6 percent—and the year's industrial growth rate—6.8 percent—indicated a steep drop in performance of Taiwan's economy. From 1979 to 1982, economic growth in Taiwan sadly fell to an average annual rate of 5.9 percent and its annual industrial growth to a meager 3.2 percent.

At the beginning of the 1980s, the rising protectionism in international markets and the increasing competition from other Asian developing nations such as Thailand and China for Taiwan's market share of low-cost manufacturing products pressured Taiwan's industry to change. Soon government officials reached a strategic consensus to develop those industries which produced high value-added goods, with the expectation of raising the value of the exports. The strategy was based on the rationale that exporting higher value products would offset the loss of export volume which had occurred as a result of the reduced import quotas to U.S. and Western European markets. It would also take Taiwan out of fierce competition with other Asian developing countries for the market share of low-cost manufacturing products. It was for this reason that Taiwan decided to develop "strategic industries," industries that currently do not occupy important positions in the total makeup of Taiwan's industry. Yet their anticipated growth is expected to generate a series of backward supply chain reactions that will create a new wave of growth of high value-added industries in Taiwan.

With this changing emphasis, industrialization in Taiwan began a new stage—the development of high tech industry. Targeting strategic industries for development was based on a list of criteria: the projected international market for the products, the strength and potential in generating backward and forward supply chain reactions in industry, the total amount of added values of the products, and the estimated level of energy consumption and environmental threats. To promote the development of strategic industries, the government established funding for venture capital, financed high-level research and development projects, and offered elaborate management and marketing assistance. Mostly the mechanical engineering and computer electronics industries were selected for development as strategic industries. In 1982 strategic industries started to show encouraging signs of growth. Some of them had already generated backward supply linkages; their demands for materials and parts created new industries on the island.

In addition to strategic industries, the government also selected eight high tech industries for intensive development in the 1980s. Each of these eight areas had potential to solve specific economic development problems in Taiwan. In 1980 energy, metallurgy, information technology, and manufacturing automation were chosen. The energy industry was selected because of Taiwan's heavy dependency on foreign energy supplies, a dependence that had been subjecting Taiwan's industry to the fluctuation of the supply and price of foreign oil. It was clear that Taiwan needed to develop alternative forms of energy. The metallurgy industry was selected because Taiwan's industry had to reduce its dependence on imported metallurgical materials. The obvious importance of information technology in today's science, engineering, and business justified its selection. The manufacturing automation technology industry was chosen to solve the problem of rising labor cost in Taiwan.

Later on, the genetic engineering industry was added to the list because of its revolutionary status in science. The study of hepatitis was also included because the disease had been epidemic on Taiwan. Laser technology's close technological link with information technology and manufacturing automation technology justified the selection of that technology. The last area added to the list was food technology, based on its expected beneficial effect on the health of Taiwan's 19 million residents. To aid the research and development activities of these high tech industries, a number of existing research institutes were identified as supporting institutes, and new research institutes were also built. To attract investments in the new high tech industry and to speed up progress, in 1973 the government began building an expensive, government-funded research institute, the Industrial Technology Research Institute, and in 1980 a huge industrial park, the Science Park in Sintsu.

One mission of the Industrial Technology Research Institute is to monitor the development of new technologies in industrial nations, to identify those that are essential to Taiwan's high tech industry, and to arrange the transfer of these technologies to Taiwan. A less glamorous mission is to conduct research and testing for industry. This function makes it the central research center of Taiwan's industries. The institute was furnished with first-rate equipment and staffed with the best scientists and engineers available; many of its staff members had studied and worked in the United States. The current president of the institute, Dr. Morris Chang, served as a vice president at Texas Instruments for many years and later held a similar position at General Dynamics. The institute filled the long-standing void in Taiwan's industry for an advanced research and development facility and capability. Since its founding in 1973, five research divisions and two research centers have been established in the institute: the Chemical, Electronics, Materials, Mechanics, and the Division for Energy and Mining Research and the Center for Measurement and Standards, and the Center for Electro-Optics and Peripherals. The Electronics Research Division is the largest division in terms of the number of personnel it commands and the most distinguished in terms of the publicity its research projects have attracted. The division was singlehandedly responsible for the birth of Taiwan's integrated circuit (IC) industry.

The IC industry shines as a successful example of Taiwan's attempt to develop new high tech industry. Prior to the birth of Taiwan's IC industry, the capacity of its electronics industry was limited to electronics component assembly, a technology introduced to Taiwan in 1966 when foreign corporations started to set up electronic component assembly plants there. Corporations such as General Instruments, Texas Instruments, and Philips brought IC packaging, testing, and quality control technology to Taiwan. However, with regard to the IC design and manufacturing technology, Taiwan had only started to experiment with them during the early 1960s when the Transportation University (Chia Tung University) established the island's first electronic engineering graduate program with a concentration on IC technology. In 1965 the university produced Taiwan's first laboratory-made IC chip. The students of this graduate program were the island's first group of individuals trained in IC technology, and made great contributions to the development of Taiwan's IC industry. In fact, most of the island's IC companies were founded and owned by these graduates.

In the early 1970s, the government decided to push for the development of Taiwan's IC industry. Accordingly, the government funded and operated an IC experimental manufacturing plant, shouldering the financial risks usually involved in pioneering a new industry. Once the experimental manufacturing plant became successful in production and operation, the whole package of technologies and experience involved in setting and operating the plant was scheduled to be transferred to the private sector. Then the government would assist interested IC manufacturers in obtaining credits, and would support their IC operation with technical and management consulting services. In the meantime, the Industrial Technology Research Institute was expected to continue its IC research and development function to encourage the industry's continuing progress and growth.

By 1976 the institute, with the help of a number of overseas Chinese IC experts, decided on the technology development direction for Taiwan's IC industry: it selected a special line of IC technology in which the industry would develop expertise, and it determined the criteria for selecting a U.S. company from which to license such a line of technology.[12] Among a total of eight U.S. corporate license proposals, RCA's CMOS technology was selected. During the next two years, the institute constructed the island's first IC experimental manufacturing plant, finished equipping the facility, and then went on to produce the first group of prototype IC chips. During these two years, the institute recruited three young, accomplished IC technology engineers from the United States, all of whom had coincidentally earned their Ph.D's from Princeton University. They made important contributions to IC technology and are among the leaders of this technology in Taiwan. Dr. C. T. Shih, vice president of the institute, currently heads the Electronics Division. By the second quarter of 1978, the quality of the IC chips produced at the experimental manufacturing plant had reached the standard agreed on in the license contract with RCA. Thus, the technical assistance received from RCA under the license agreement had been completed.

During the second half of 1979, the Ministry of Economic Affairs instructed the research institute to begin its second major IC development project. The goals set for the project were (1) to upgrade the IC design, testing, and application capability, (2) to integrate CAD (computer-aided design) technology with the IC designing process, (3) to develop mask manufacturing capability, (4) to develop very large-sized integrated circuit (VLIS) manufacturing technology, and (5) to transfer the research institute's IC technology to the private sector and to assist the development of the IC industry. In 1979 Taiwan's first private IC manufacturer came into existence. At the time, however, other than those who worked at the research institute, Taiwan had few IC technology engineers. The government, anxious to effect the successful transfer of IC technology to the private sector, arranged the transfer of some of the institute's IC engineers to the manufacturer. The manufacturer was therefore able to make rapid progress in business as well as technology.

In 1987 the island's second IC manufacturing corporation, ISMC, was established. It also recruited its technical personnel from the research institute. The growing business of these two IC corporations brought into existence a number of IC design companies, every one of which was founded by former employers of the research institute. Soon, Fairchild, Texas Instruments, and NEC had also set up their IC design operations in Taiwan. To promote further progress, the research institute provided heavy technical assistance to the industry in the technological areas that were considered to be important to future growth—the mask manufacturing technology and the integration of CAD technology with the design of the application-specific integrated circuit. As indicated in a self-appraisal of the research institute recorded in the 1988 Electronics Division Report, the quality of the IC chips produced in Taiwan had reached above the 20 percentile mark among the IC chips produced in the world. Such accomplishments allowed the Taiwanese to rightfully claim that the island's IC industry had been solidly established.

The Science Park in Sintsu was founded in 1980. It was inspired by the government's earlier successful endeavor, the Export Processing Zone, where the government purchased land, put up roads and utilities, set up supporting and management services, built housing facilities, and invited investors to establish manufacturing operations in the processing zone. Unlike the earlier established Export Processing Zone, only high tech corporations were allowed to operate in the park. The government, seeking to attract foreign investors and overseas Chinese entrepreneurs to establish high tech businesses in the park, offered them low interest loans and generous tax advantages. The park was specifically located in the neighborhood of the Industrial Technology Research Institute and two leading technology universities in order to make research and development facilities and services conveniently available to high tech corporations in the park. According to an 1989 report, eighty-five high tech corporations were operating in the park, and, based on the values of the products exported, the park had an average annual growth rate of 100 percent.

Since the early 1970s, both the government and the industry have recognized the urgent need for industry to surpass its specialization in low-cost and low-technology manufacturing. To address this need, the government set up a number of programs and received good responses from the industry. In this effort, the government demonstrated a remarkable ingenuity in policymaking, and in return, the industry showed its own brand of creativity, diligence, and resolve. Together they were able to accomplish impressive technological progress. The ambition, hard drive, and the eventual brilliant success of Acer Group, the Taiwan-based computer manufacturer, perhaps epitomized industry's leap forward to high tech fields. In 1976 the founder of the company, Stanley Shih, one of the first group of graduates from the electronics engineering graduate program at the Transportation University, together with his wife and three other young engineers, started the company with a capital of U.S. $25,000 and with five years of work experience in the electronics engineering field.[13]

At the time, Taiwan did not have computer manufacturing capability. In 1980 electronic games played on standalone game machines became a vogue in Taiwan and gave rise to a number of electronic game machine manufacturers. Because of the illegal activities spawned by electronic game parlors, the government banned the playing of the game. With the banning many electronic game machine manufacturers imported and marketed Apple computers as their new line of business. This allowed them to capitalize their trade knowledge with the electronic products, as well as their familiarity with the electronic game player market. These manufacturers soon discovered many similarities between the electronic game machines they had manufactured and the personal computers they were marketing—a mother board with IC chips and some electronic components enclosed in a box connected with a monitor and a keyboard. Since the industry in Taiwan had years of experience with assembling electronic products, these manufacturers believed that the industry could assemble microcomputers by using imported components. Thus, these manufacturers began to produce counterfeited Apple II microcomputers on the island. At the same time, the company founded by Stanley Shih imported and marketed microprocessors to supplement its microprocessor learning-kit manufacturing business.

In October 1981 the company produced its first-generation microcomputer, the Microprofessor I, a microcomputer distinguished by its use of a small display panel instead of a regular-sized monitor. In 1983 the company put out its second-generation microcomputer, Microprofessor II, using a microprocessor compatible with that of Apple II. However, the already low-priced Microprofessor II was not a strong competitor of the counterfeited Apple II in Taiwan's computer market. In addition to Microprofessor II's soft position in pricing, it was less than 100 percent compatible with Apple II. Thus, some of the software developed for Apple II could not run on Microprofessor II, even though it offered more computing power than Apple II. Nevertheless, Microprofessor II's sales volume was acceptable. By the time the much improved Microprofessor III, equipped with an 8088 microprocessor, hit the market in 1984, the manufacturers of the counterfeited Apple II had been sued by Apple for infringing on its patent rights. This legal action stopped their production in Taiwan. The withdrawal of the counterfeited microcomputers from the market allowed Microprofessor III to take over a significant portion of the microcomputer market in Taiwan. With this development the company began its long, remarkable growth, often with an average annual growth rate of 250 percent.

The Acer Group's experience indicates the typical obstacles that aspiring high tech industries have had to overcome in Taiwan. The first obstacle was the industry's lag behind the state of art technology and its limited access to high tech information. Foreign firms, foreign suppliers, and Western-educated engineers and scientists transmitted the latest technologies to Taiwan. Before founding his company, Stanley Shih, had worked for two electronics companies on Taiwan, both of which were operated by Western-educated engineers. Based on this work experience he learned the electronic calculator design and manufacturing technology that later became the technical base of his company's early computer manufacturing business. Undeniably, his company also benefited from the technologies brought to Taiwan by foreign firms, most notably General Dynamics, RCA, and Philips. In the early 1980s Multitech, the former entity of Acer, contracted a dealership with a number of U.S.microprocessor and electronics manufacturers. The dealership with foreign electronic firms must have helped the company acquire the latest electronic technology.

The second obstacle to high tech companies in Taiwan involved the size of the domestic market for high tech products: it was too small to lend sufficient initial support to new high tech industries. Except for those companies that had manufacturing contracts with foreign companies and were thus guaranteed a certain amount of international sales, new high tech companies found it difficult to sustain their businesses soley on the basis of manufacturing. To overcome this difficulty, high tech manufacturers usually contracted dealerships with foreign companies on products related to their own to take advantage of overlapping markets and technologies, as did Multitech during its early years. Another often used tactic was to bid for manufacturing contracts with foreign companies on products close to their own. For a long time, Multitech, while manufacturing its own brand-name microcomputers, was also under manufacturing contract with a number of U.S. computer manufacturers to produce its microcomputers and computer components.

The third obstacle had to do with dealing with a market that was completely ignorant of their products. When these companies first introduced their products to the island's market, they often found that they had to invest in the education of their users. Educating consumers of high tech products can be expensive. When Multitech first introduced Microprofessor I to the Taiwanese market, Stanley Shih immediately realized that it would be necessary to train the users of the computer and to publish computer literature. Therefore, he founded a computer training school that currently has branches throughout Taiwan. He also founded a number of computer journals that serviced different groups of computer users. These journals were so successful that he formed a publication company specialized in computer-related literature. Even he may have been surprised by the volume and profits of his publication business.

The last obstacle to the aspiring Taiwanese high tech corporations was as follows: the growth of these companies had often been limited by the restricted trade quotas applied to their export markets and the obvious difficulties involved in servicing their foreign customers. To pave the way to unlimited future growth in export markets, in 1987 the Acer Group acquired a California-based computer company, Counterpoint. The acquisition gave the company membership in the U.S. computer manufacturing community as well as unlimited access to the vast U.S. microcomputer market.

In the last few years, the industry in Taiwan has made a number of significant moves to adjust to the changing international trade environment: the 40 percent appreciation of the Taiwan currency in the last four years as against the U.S. dollar; increasing U.S. pressure for balanced trade and the resulting tightening trade quotas for Taiwanese products exported to the United States; and the formation of the European Common Market. To counter the rising production costs resulting from the currency appreciation and to get around the tightening trade quotas to the U.S. markets, the aggressive owners of labor-intensive manufacturing industries, such as footwear and textiles, relocated, or planned to relocate, their plants to Thailand, China, the Philippines, and Malaysia to take advantage of the low-cost labor and unused trade quotas available in these countries. The exodus of Taiwanese light industries to these areas is expected to continue as long as these countries extend invitations to Taiwanese industries and as long as the high labor cost in Taiwan continues to dictate such a move.

With regard to those businesses that chose to stay in Taiwan, the government urged immediate product upgrading to increase the added value of their products. The government also encouraged light industry business owners to form trading companies to handle the marketing and sales of their products in the international market to replace the services that had long been provided by foreign trading firms. These owners could therefore save commission payments and perhaps even make some additional profits from themselves handling product sales in the overseas market. The government has advised the industry to diversify its export markets—to move away from their overconcentration on the U.S. market, to increase sales in the Japanese and Western European markets, and to open up markets in Eastern Europe and Russia. The government is also encouraging the high tech industry to set up sales operations or manufacturing plants in countries where their products have been well marketed. For instance, the government has negotiated an agreement with the government of Ireland to establish an industrial park in that country to manufacture microcomputers for the upcoming European Common Market. An outstanding successful example of expanding Taiwanese business to foreign countries is Formosa Plastics, Inc., which currently has six plants operating in the United States and in 1989, for the first time, made the list of *Fortune* 500 companies.

NOTES

1. Richard Barrett and Soomi Chin, "Export-Oriented States in the World System," in Frederick Deyo, ed., *The Political Economy of the New Asian Industrialism* (Ithaca, N.Y.: Cornell University Press, 1987), p. 24.

2. Ching-Yuan Lin, *Industrialization in Taiwan, 1946–1972* (New York: Praeger, 1973), p. 15.

3. Ibid., p. 17.

4. George Barclay, *Colonial Development and Population in Taiwan* (Port Washington, N.Y.: Kennikat Press, 1972), p. 136.

5. Lin, *Industrialization in Taiwan*, p. 19.

6. S. C. Hsieh and T. H. Lee, *Agricultural Development and Its Contribution to Economic Growth in Taiwan* (Taipei: Chinese American Joint Commission on Rural Reconstruction, 1966), Economic Digest Series No. 17, p. 103.

7. "The Evolution of Taiwan's Economy During the Japanese Period," Taiwan Economic History Series No. 2 (Taipei: Bank of Taiwan Publication, 1955), p. 97.

8. Executive Yuan, Council on Economic Development, *The Journey of the Modernization of Taiwan's Economy* (Taipei: Bureau of Economic Research, 1987), p. 25.

9. Ibid., p. 2.

10. Materials on the evolution of the industrialization in Taiwan are based on Wen-Pau Chang, "The First Sixteen Years of Industrialization in Taiwan," in *Research Report on Taiwan's Economy* (Taipei: Ministry of Economic Affairs Publication, 1965), pp. 266–284.

11. Some of these projects had already been underway, though on a much smaller scale.

12. For detailed information on the history of the development of the island's IC technology, see Sean-Ming Lin, *A Study of the Development Process of New Industries in Developing Countries: A Case Study of the IC Industry in Taiwan* (Taiwan: National Taiwan University Press, 1987).

13. Bio-Lu Wang, *The Charm of a High Rate of Growth: The History of the Success of a Computer Giant* (Taipei: Time Publishing, 1988) was the source of the development history of the Acer Group.

8   INTERNATIONAL TRADE

The long-term, steady growth of a small island economy such as Taiwan's depends heavily on its foreign trade performance. Since the 1960s, its economy has experienced vigorous growth, based chiefly on the rapid, steady expansion of its international trade. In 1989 Taiwan was the world's sixteenth largest trading country and eleventh in volume exported. It ranked next to Canada in volume exported, which is an impressive performance for a country the size of Rhode Island. With its trade surplus of U.S. $19.03 million in 1987 and U.S. $1,444 million of foreign exchange reserves in 1989, for example, Taiwan has come a long way from its early years. For instance, it recorded a trade deficit of U.S. $83.99 million and a meager foreign exchange reserve of U.S. $1.62 million in 1953, the first year the government started to record the island's trade statistics.[1]

Taiwan's economic policies before 1960 did not reflect a policy of growth in foreign trade. In fact, during the first ten years of the Nationalist administration, rampant inflation, large government budget deficits, low foreign exchange reserves, and the need to feed the large influx of refugees forced the government to take an inward approach to the island's economy, namely, an import-substitution strategy. A number of economists raised questions concerning the government's early economic approach. They wondered whether an outward approach to expand the island's exports would yield quicker results for the economy. It should be pointed out that the government's choice of inward approach had to do with the traditionally land-bound mentality of the Chinese. Psychologically, the Chinese felt more secure with a self-sufficient agricultural and industrial production. Time and time again in Chinese history this psychological security has been proven central to China's social and political stability.

Taiwan's import substitution strategy demanded high tariffs and other import restriction measures to discourage imports deemed to be in direct competition with the products of import-substituting industries. In addition, a multiple foreign exchange rate was imposed to give favorable exchange rates to importing raw materials and equipment to be used for import-substituting industries and to penalize the import of finished goods considered to be in competition with the products of import-substituting industries. The multiple foreign exchange rate system artifically lowered the product cost of import-substituting industries while inflating the cost of imported equivalents. Moreover, during the import substitution period, sugar- and rice-exporting farmers were heavily taxed by an unfavorable foreign exchange rate applied to their export earnings. Thus, the farmers in effect subsidized the import substitution's policy. After the U.S. aid to Taiwan bailed out Taiwan's economy from double-digit inflation and the accumulated government budget deficits, the aid money was lavishly used to subsidize the island's import substitution industry.

During the import substitution period, rice, sugar, and other agricultural products made up one-half the island's total exports, while fertilizer, cotton, wheat, soybeans, and capital equipment were the major import items. Japan was the major export market of Taiwanese products; between 40 and 50 percent of all exports went to Japan. Products from the United States and Japan were Taiwan's leading imports, more than 40 percent of Taiwan's imports came from the United States, and Japanese products constituted a slightly smaller percentage of Taiwan's imports.[2]

From the standpoint of foreign trade performance, the import substitution period was not a time of great importance. However, the trade policies and practices established during this period firmly shaped a number of strategies and tactics that would be followed in Taiwan's trade policies and trade-related practices. The government established its power to use tariffs, import control measures, and a multiple foreign exchange rate system as instruments to create an economic environment conducive to a desirable foreign trade orientation. The success of the import substitution policy of the 1950s reaffirmed the government's authority to use such policy instruments to effect desired responses in the economy. In the following decade, the government demonstrated an even more forceful and skillful utilization of these policy instruments to create a healthy economic environment for the export industries.

During this period, Taiwan's manufacturers adopted a dual business function, manufacturing and international trade, and thus established a business operation model for manufacturers who followed. During the import substitution period, importers of industrial raw materials, machinery, and equipment enjoyed privileged import duty rates and foreign exchange certificates. The combined effect of these two privileges alone could bring importers handsome business profits. For this reason, most of the island's manufacturers expanded their businesses to include an international trade operation. Even today an industrial establishment on Taiwan commonly leads this dual function.

The business operation of the Acer Group serves as a good example of this dual business function. This practice produced a huge number of small international trading establishments covering every conceivable line of import and export in the economy. This development precluded any attempt to establish large, single-purpose trading companies on the island. Because of obvious financial and resource constraints, Taiwan's small trading companies were unable to function effectively in the international market. Compared to those super Japanese trading houses which operated with a wealth of resources, the operations of the Taiwanese trading firms in the international market suffered from insufficient resources and thus noncompetitiveness. The 40 percent currency appreciation and the tightening U.S. import quotas represent a challenge to the Taiwanese to apply innovative marketing and sales tactics to their foreign trade. This demands the founding of supersized trading companies that have the resources and capabilities to meet these challenges.

During the import substitution period, the country's industrial development policies and its trade policies were closely coordinated. Industries targeted for development during this period were protected against foreign competition by a combination of high tariffs and various import control policy measures. Import tax rebates and favorable foreign exchange rates were accorded to importers of industrial materials, equipment, and machinery. Following the import-substitution period, a different type of industry was targeted for development at each industrialization stage. However, the country's import and export policies had always been quickly adjusted to lend support to any new development orientation.

Applications for import and export licenses, duties, quotas, and foreign exchanges were once so complicated and trivial that the government finally had to establish special offices to handle applications, and businesses had to hire specialized personnel to take charge of them. Firms were established to assist business clients to file applications. A major attraction of the Export Processing Zones to entrepreneurs was the service provided at the zone to handle these applications. Later, when the Science Park was built, the plan included a provision that this service be offered at the park.

During the import substitution period, the supply of foreign exchange was meager. The government decided to control outbound foreign exchanges by regulating the amount of foreign exchange issued to individual persons or businesses. Even though foreign exchange regulations were abolished in 1987, the nearly forty years of government control of foreign exchange resulted in a gigantic accumulation of foreign exchange reserves. These reserves had now become a burden to the government.

Soon after the import substitution policy was in full force, the limited-sized Taiwan market became saturated with the products of import substitution industries. An estimate of the utilization of plant capacity taken in 1955 indicates that industries in general did not operate at full capacity; some of them only operated at 25 percent capacity. To solve this problem, the government naturally changed its trade policies to promote exports. In July 1955 the government promulgated tax rebate regulations to encourage export activities. Under these regulations, imported industrial materials and equipment to be used for manufacturing products for export became eligible for rebates of import duties, and defense and commodity taxes. To the contrary of what the government had anticipated, the response to this incentive measure was not satisfactory; export activities had shown little improvement.

According to K. H. Wu, the founder and deputy chairman of the China External Trade Development Council, business gave this weak response because at the time the Taiwanese had little knowledge of international trade and the international market. Their only foreign trade information came from their business contacts with Japanese traders. To better inform Taiwanese businesspeople about international trade and the market, the government regularly organized business tours to visit foreign countries and study other business ideas and market opportunities. On one of these trips Wu came upon the idea of establishing Taiwan's frozen seafood processing industry. When he returned from the trip, he recommended setting up such an industry in Taiwan. Later he became the first president of the government-owned frozen seafood processing company.

During the second half of the 1950s, the oversaturated market and the underutilized industry demanded quick changes in economic policies. Between 1958 and 1960, the government instituted a number of reform measures to improve the investment environment. Under the Statute for the Encouragement of Business Investment, qualified industrial establishments could enjoy a five-year tax holiday as well as exemptions of import duties on machinery and equipment. The promulgation of the

Program for Foreign Exchange Adjustments and Trade Control Reductions in April 1958 officially marked the beginning of the new export-oriented growth era of Taiwan's economy. This program and many of its later revisions consisted of major changes of laws and regulations in three areas. The first area involved the devaluation of the overvalued local currency and the abandonment of the multiple exchange rate in favor of a unified, stable exchange rate (new Taiwan dollar)—N.T. $40.00 to U.S. $1.00.[3] The currency was devalued in order to increase the competitiveness of Taiwan's products in the international market. A unified, stable foreign exchange rate allowed the Taiwan businessperson to make reliable business analyses and to remove the uncertain element involved in computing business profits.

A second area involved tariff reduction and the relaxation of control over foreign exchange allocations. The import quota system established in the previous period for controlling the import of commodities was first liberated and later totally abolished. Restrictions placed on importing raw materials, machinery, and equipment began to be relaxed in 1958. Import restrictions on controlled goods were also relaxed. On the other hand, qualifications for domestic industries to apply for trade protection were tightened up. Manufacturers who applied for trade protection were asked to prove that both their product quality and production capacity could fully satisfy the domestic market demand and that the required imported raw materials for production had not exceeded 70 percent of the total production cost. In addition, the factory price of the product applying for protection should not be more than 25 percent higher than the market price of its import equivalent. This figure was lowered to 15 percent in 1964, to 10 percent in 1968, and to 5 percent in 1973.

The third area involved the institution of major export promotion policy measures. In addition to rebates of customs duties and commodity taxes on imported raw materials designated for export production, manufacturers of export products were qualified for exemptions from business and stamp taxes as well as an additional 2 percent deduction from total annual taxable income. A 10 percent tax deduction was given to manufacturing, mining, and handicraft businesses that in previous years had exported 50 percent or more of their output. Export manufacturers were allowed to keep the foreign exchange earned from importing raw materials and equipment or to sell their foreign exchange privileges to others for profits. Special low interest loans were made available to these manufacturers for purchasing raw materials and insurance. Manufacturers of textiles, canned mushrooms, canned asparagus spears, and citronella oil were encouraged to form individual trade associations to regulate export volume and to unify pricing. Trade associations of cotton spinning, steel and iron, rubber products, monosodium glutamate, woolens and fabrics, and paper and paper products manufacturers began to subsidize their exports by charging higher prices on their products sold on domestic markets.

Overall, the government responded swiftly in instituting mechanisms and building an economic environment conducive to the growth of exports. In 1970 the government approved a levy of 0.625 percent of the declared value of the island's exported products to finance the Fund for the Promotion and Expansion of Exports which is the funding source of the famous quasi-government export promotion agency—the China External Trade Development Council. The agency's services included inspections of export products, trade, technical and management consultations, market research and information, and the sponsorship of international trade shows and exhibits. The Export Processing Zone is another example of the government's ingenuity in promoting export trade.

The worldwide oil shortages of the 1970s changed the course of Taiwan's economic growth. Beginning in 1973, the recession and inflation that affected its trading partners adversely affected Taiwan's own economy. The quadrupled petroleum prices alone with a raw material shortage in the world market sent prices up both rapidly and steadily. In addition, the island experienced a fast money expansion between 1973 and 1974. It fueled the already high inflation on the island. In January 1974 the government adopted a number of strong anti-inflation measures. By applying a large-scale, across-the-board increase to bank interests and a one-time substantial price raise to government-controlled goods and services such as petroleum products and electric power, the government soon stabilized prices. The subsequent decline of international prices on raw materials and foods, the sudden shift of Taiwan's trade from surplus to deficit, and the accumulated government budget surplus—all contributed to stabilizing the island's economy following the first worldwide oil crisis.

With regard to the inflationary effect that a huge trade surplus could have on the economy, the government began to try to reduce export incentives. The program whereby capital was lent to exporters based solely on credits established through previous trade performances was discontinued. Thenceforth, preshipment preferential export credits were granted only to exporters able to present buyers' letters of credits. Stricter qualifications for rebates of custom duties were enforced. The inflation and recession that set in after the first oil crisis began to level off in mid-1975.

Starting from the fourth quarter of 1977, the economy showed a marked improvement. In 1978 the Japanese yen experienced a sharp appreciation, which helped to increase the competitiveness of Taiwanese products on the Japanese market. The Taiwanese seized the opportunity to expand their exports to Japan; the expansion brought about a significant increase in the island's industrial production which had in turn accelerated GNP growth. That year Taiwan had a trade surplus of U.S. $16.6 billion. Later, Taiwan's trade surplus was substantially modified by a sharp increase of Taiwan's imports coming from the skyrocketing oil prices following the second oil crisis in 1979. However, Taiwan's exports of the following year were robust, registering a trade surplus of U.S. $14.1 billion. In 1982 the island's trade surplus rose to U.S. $33 billion. The recovery of the world's economy, especially the U.S. economy in 1983 and 1984, boosted the island's exports. At the same time investments in industry experienced a slowdown that caused a low growth in imports. In 1983 Taiwan had a trade surplus of $48.3 billion, in 1984 the figure had climbed to U.S. $85 billion; in 1985 to U.S. $106 billion; and in 1986 to U.S. $156 billion. The continuing growth of Taiwan's trade surplus with the United States had become a burden to the government in Taiwan.[4]

Aside from forces in the international market that favored growth in exports, a number of persistent, unique characteristics of Taiwan's export industries and businesses were also responsible for the remarkable performance of its exports since the 1960s. These characteristics were: planned structural changes of the product composition of the exports, rapid and responsive institutional adjustments to the changing direction of the exports, and the coming of age of Taiwan's knowledge and skills in international trade.

The country's intense dedication to expanding its exports since the 1960s can be readily discerned in the ever present propaganda slogan of the island—"everything is for export." The slogan appeared on highway billboards, street signposts, government buildings, and the advertisement section of newspapers and magazines. It expresses the commitment as well as the expectation of the Taiwanese. This commitment to exports bred a unique foreign trade practice; that is, contrary to the normal progression from domestic products to export items observed in industrial nations, the majority of Taiwan's export products were developed, manufactured for, and sold only on the export markets. This practice began in the 1950s when the farmers started to grow cash crops targeted solely for foreign consumption. In the 1960s, the Taiwanese manufacturers began to display the same kind of responsiveness and flexibility as did the Taiwanese farmers in the 1950s, making product adjustments to the changing demands in the international market. In developing new products for export, however, the Taiwanese manufacturers experienced a similar difficulty as did the Taiwanese farmers. The limited size of the consumer market alone did not justify the cost involved in developing new products. Therefore, most of the successful export products did not grow out of domestically consumed products; instead, they were designed and manufactured specifically for the export markets. Government policies for promoting exports had been so effective that more profits could actually be made from exporting the products than selling them on the domestic market.

Until recent years, industrial products exported from Taiwan have largely been developed from products originally manufactured in Taiwan for export under foreign contracts in which foreign firms provide product designs and manufacturing drawings, and in many cases, even product components and technical assistance. Through these manufacturing contracts, production technology as well as international market information and contacts were transferred to Taiwan. The knowledge and skills that the Taiwanese acquired through these contracts greatly contributed to the development and growth of most of Taiwan's leading export industries, such as consumer electronics, machinery, tools, yacht building, sporting goods, furniture, textile, toys, and footwear. In fact, during the 1960s and early 1970s, manufacturing contracts with foreign firms were the major cause of the booming expansion of Taiwan's exports. Economists observed that the comparative advantage factor forced a distribution pattern of the developing nations' products in the international markets: these nations tended to product labor-intensive products for markets in the developed nations and capital- and technology-intensive products for consumption in developing nations. This was exactly the case with the distribution of the Taiwanese products. The United States, Western Europe, and Japan were the markets for its labor-intensive products, and Hong Kong and the Southeast Asian countries were the markets for its capital- and technology-intensive products.

In 1970 the China External Trade Development Council was founded as Taiwan's central trade promotion agency. Currently, it has offices in 139 cities throughout the world. In countries with no formal diplomatic ties with Taiwan, these offices conveniently served the commerce function of an embassy. These offices usually provided liaisons between Taiwanese businesses and the business community in the host country, gathered business information and data about the host country and forwarded them back home, and assisted the Taiwanese businesses and industries to participate in trade shows and industrial exhibits held in the host country. At the present time, the agency employs about four thousand people worldwide. Its administrative structure includes six divisions: market information, market research, trade show, commercial design, packaging design, and training. The Divisions of Commercial Design and Packaging Design were newly added, their missions being to help Taiwan's export businesses improve their product appearance and packaging technology as part of the effort to increase the international competitiveness of Taiwanese products. The Training Division regularly offers courses on international business investments, management, bank loans and credits, business law, and a host of selected technical subject areas. It also runs an intensive management training school for top business executives. Because Taiwan's export businesses tend to be small or medium in size, they do not usually have a full-fledged international marketing and sales function, nor do they fully appreciate the business value of these functions. Services provided by the agency make up what these businesses fail to provide for themselves.[5]

Two international developments in the 1980s presented difficult challenges to Taiwan's export businesses. The first developed the 40 percent appreciation of the Taiwanese currency in a period of four years. This served as a paralyzing blow to Taiwan's exports for their competitiveness had rested on their winning low prices. In responding to the sudden change, the Taiwanese export businesses cut their profit margins to offer unchanged price quotations, with the hope of retaining export markets in order to continue to run a fully utilized production facility. In the meantime, they expected their efforts at production automation and product upgrading to allow them to regain their lost profit margins.

The second development was Taiwan's persistent trade surplus with the United States. (In fact, the 1989 U.S. trade deficit with Taiwan was only smaller than that with Japan.) This surplus forced the U.S. government to exert pressures on Taiwan to voluntarily curtail its export expansion to the U.S. market and to limit the increase of the assigned import quotas to Taiwan. Because Taiwanese exports to the United States constituted about 42.5 percent of the island's total exports in the last few years, restraints on Taiwan's exports to the United States could significantly disturb the island's export businesses. To deal with the imminent threat to exports, the government recommended product upgrade and export market diversification. When the value of the export products was increased as the expected result of product upgrade, the total value of the island's exports would be increased without raising the total number of exported items. This strategy would permit a continuing expansion of Taiwan's exports to the United States even under constrained U.S. import quotas. Taiwan's serious efforts to diversify its export markets led to the establishment of business ties with countries with which trade had previously been banned for political reasons, such as Eastern European countries and Russia.

To meet the challenges which the international developments of the 1980s brought to their foreign trade, the Taiwanese adopted a number of fundamental changes in trade practice. The very trade strategy of manufacturing foreign companies' products under contracts, though it had earlier brought an export boom to Taiwan, became a threat to the future of Taiwan's foreign trade. In the 1960s manufacturing contracts with foreign corporations gave rise to a large number of industries and businesses and were responsible for the rapid expansion of Taiwan's exports. The island's low-cost, disciplined labor, the extraordinary entrepreneurial spirit of Taiwan's business owners, and the government's strong support to foreign investments and new industries had indeed attracted foreign corporations to contract product manufacturing in Taiwan. With its recent 40 percent currency appreciation, however, the country lost its long-standing competitive advantages in labor cost and therefore risked losing a good portion of its export businesses.

The government recommended two strategies to counter this threat: (1) instead of continuing manufacturing products for foreign corporations, the Taiwanese were encouraged to develop, manufacture, and market their own export products, and (2) the labor-intensive industries—textiles, toys, sporting goods, apparel, and footwear—were all encouraged to relocate plants in other developing countries to take advantage of those countries' low labor cost and unused trade quotas. As for those industries that chose to stay, the Bureau of Industrial Development, a newly established agency in the Ministry of Economic Affairs, was assigned to assist them in developing new products with high added values.

The bureau selected a number of industries, including automobile, electronics, machinery, and tools, for development as future export industries. Through developing, manufacturing, and marketing their own export products, the Taiwanese may gain a bigger share of profits than manufacturing products under foreign contracts in which they only earn manufacturing profits. The Taiwanese recognize that while their manufacturing technology and product quality cannot be faulted, they need to improve their skills in product development and marketing. They have been improving their skills in these areas and have already made some progress.

Government in Asian countries such as Thailand, the Philippines, Malaysia, and Indonesia, where labor costs are low and trade quotas are available, welcomed the relocation of the Taiwanese manufacturing plants in their countries. Since the beginning of the great exodus of the Taiwanese labor-intensive manufacturers in the mid-1980s, these countries have received the largest number of relocated plants. Some relocated manufacturers have already experienced success at their new locations. This move has proved to be a viable solution to manufacturers' difficulties resulting from the currency appreciation and tightened up trade quotas.

Another Taiwanese trade practice that required immediate and fundamental changes was the heavy dependency of Taiwanese exports on foreign governments' trade quotas. Quotas for importing goods into the United States and Western European countries (the two major export markets of Taiwanese products), where the sentiment of protectionism runs high, was of particular concern to the Taiwanese. The expansion of the economy relied on the growth of exports. Thus, restrained trade quotas meant restricted economic growth. A strategy developed to counter international protectionism was to manufacture products in or near their export markets. Plans were developed to set up industrial parks on the Mexican border to the United States, in the Caribbean countries, in the United States such as the state of Arizona, and in Ireland to house Taiwanese manufacturers.

A third Taiwanese trade practice requiring changes was the dependency of Taiwan's exports on the U.S. market. The fact that nearly half of all Taiwanese exports went to the U.S. market allowed the United States to have a dominant influence over Taiwan's economy. The aftermath of the sudden sharp appreciation of the Taiwanese currency, together with the tightening up of U.S. import quotas, taught the Taiwanese the important lesson that an economy should not lean too heavily on foreign economies as did the Taiwanese on the U.S. economy. Therefore, plans were drawn up to diversify Taiwan's export markets. These plans called for an increased emphasis on the Western European market. The China External Trade Development Council has since increased its presence in Western Europe. A number of super warehouses were set up at the strategic trading points in Western Europe to help promote Taiwanese trade on the continent. Trade with the Mideast and Africa was also stepped up, and markets in the Eastern European countries and Russia were explored. To facilitate a two-way trade with the Eastern European countries, the Taiwanese government helped these countries set up trade offices in Taiwan. The Taiwanese government sought opportunities for economic cooperation with those Eastern European countries that underwent political transformation. Contacts have recently been made with the government in Hungary.

Perhaps the most remarkable development in Taiwan's pursuit of new export markets is the establishment of an indirect trade relation with mainland China who had been Taiwan's threat and inplacable enemy for the last forty years. Many believed that the pressure of finding export markets for Taiwan's products had forced the late President Chiang Chien-Kuo in 1987 to abolish the government's forty-year ban on any form of contact with the mainland. In fact, before the official approval of indirect trade relations with the mainland, underground commerce between Taiwan and the mainland has been taking place for years through a third country, usually Hong Kong, Thailand, or Singapore. Although at present the government in Taiwan forbids direct business investments in the mainland's economy, observers predict that it is only a matter of time before the prohibition is lifted. Forward-looking Taiwanese entrepreneurs have already made many visits to the mainland to explore investment or joint venture opportunities.

The development of Taiwan's economy made foreign trade the life line of its economy. In the last forty years, changes in the island's industry, institutional structure, and trade practices in response to internally or externally emanating challenges strengthened the competitiveness of its export products and expanded its export markets. Taiwan's recent efforts to upgrade its industry, diversify its export markets, establish manufacturing plants in the United States, Western Europe, and places close to its major export markets, and develop its satellite economies in neighboring Asian countries suggest that a new chapter is in the making. Therefore, despite hard challenges that are presently confronting the export economy, Taiwan's foreign trade is likely to continue its remarkable growth into the future, only with more vigor and surer steps.

NOTES

1. *1989 Data Book*, Ministry of Economic Affairs, Republic of China.

2. For details on the reasoning and justifications behind Taiwan's import substitution policy, see Kwoh-Ting Li, *The Evolution of Policy Behind Taiwan's Development Success* (New Haven, Conn.: Yale University Press, 1988), pp. 101–147.

3. Executive Yuan, Council on Economic Development, *The Journey of the Modernization of Taiwan's Economy* (Taipei: Bureau of Economic Research, 1987), pp. 55–57.

4. Ibid., pp. 46–47.

5. 1989 China External Trade Development Council brochure.

9 THE MONETARY, FISCAL, AND FINANCIAL SYSTEM

Capital and other resources are, of course, important to modern economic growth in developing countries. Their capital needs usually include not only those for financing business investments leading to economic growth, but also those for payments on imports and foreign debts. However, per capita income in developing nations, in general, tend to be low, yet consumption in these countries often tends to be high. The combined result is not enough savings in the countries to satisfy their capital needs for economic development. Furthermore, since these countries tend to import more than they export, they do not have a good standing in the international credit market to secure loans for economic development projects. Under this financial constraint, a developing nation cannot easily employ monetary and fiscal policies to stimulate and accumulate savings, to facilitate economic growth, and to maintain a stable economy?

Postwar Taiwan's problem with insufficient capital had all the constraints common to developing economies. In addition to these usual difficulties, it was faced with double-digit inflation and a huge budget deficit. While the war-damaged production sector awaited reconstruction capital, two million refugees and six hundred thousand military personnel needed to be resettled. The question that naturally arises is how the Taiwanese managed to overcome all these difficulties and still accumulate enough capital to finance its economic growth and at the same time maintain its stability and effect an equal income distribution. This question is the subject of this chapter. Here we examine the evolution of Taiwan's monetary and fiscal policies over the last forty-one years. We will also study the progressive development of Taiwan's modern financial system as an instrument of mediating savings and investing capital.

Taiwan's monetary policies since 1949 have been aimed at effecting controlled inflation, public confidence in local currency, stable market prices, sufficient investment capital, a balanced government budget, and adequate foreign exchange reserves. Although industrialization and a good foreign trade performance were essential, the development of Taiwan's economy could have been severely hindered or even destroyed without a well-designed monetary policy. Taiwan's development experience indeed tested the wisdom of its monetary policies. From October 25, 1945, the day the island was retroceded to the Nationalist government, to the second half of 1950 when U.S. economic aid to Taiwan was resumed, the government's monetary policies faced the greatest challenges as instruments to economic stability. During these five years, wholesale prices increased more than one thousand times. A number of tumultuous events contributed to the enormous inflation rate—the end of World War II, the loss of the mainland, and the Nationalist retreat to Taiwan. The war crippled agriculture which had been the main source of national income. While postwar reconstruction efforts required huge sums of capital, the war-ravaged economy was unable to generate sufficient revenues, and so the government had to resort to printing monies to finance reconstruction. Surely, this action further aggravated the already severe inflation.

During this period, the monetary system was threatened by three developments. First, Taiwan had to face a rapid increase in the money supply. In just two months after retrocession, money supplies grew from a little more than 14 billion to almost 29 billion (Taiwanese dollars). On June 14, 1949, less than five years after the end of the war, money supplies reached a staggering 5,270 billion Taiwanese dollars. This amounted to a 180-fold increase in a period of only three years and seven months. The government's introduction of a new currency, the new Taiwanese dollar, was a futile attempt to curtail the growth of money supplies.

The second development was a too rapid expansion of bank deposits and loans. In order to correct the problem of low bank deposits owing to persistent, high inflation, in July 1946 the government instituted policy measures to increase the volume of bank savings. To centrally implement the savings promotion policies, it was required that all bank deposits be transferred to the Bank of Taiwan; this bank was asked to exercise the functions of a central bank in the absence of an official one. Furthermore, all banks were instructed to demand that their loan customers pay back at least 20 percent of the total amount of loans. A ceiling was placed on the amount of money that could be withdrawn from bank accounts owned by government or government-controlled businesses. All levels of central and local government were instructed to make deposits only with the Bank of Taiwan.

In August 1948 all banks were notified not to make any loans without the approval of a designated government office. In May 1949 the government enacted new bank deposit and loan regulations with the intent of controlling inflation by tightening up bank loans and attracting bank savings. However, the implementation of these policy measures led to a quite different outcome from the one that had been anticipated. Both bank loans and deposits expanded tremendously; total bank deposits increased 1,986 times while bank loans increased 1.278 times.[1] Another development was a rapidly soaring interest rate. The climbing market prices on the island drove up its interest rates. In January 1947 the interest rate on bank deposits was 4 percent, and it rose to 12 percent fourteen months later. The monthly interest rate for business loans in June 1947 was 8.5 percent, and it climbed to 81 percent only twenty-five months later.

As could be predicted, this magnitude of monetary abnormalities paralyzed the economy and caused enormous social unrest. The financially troubled government finally turned to monetary reforms and the institution of a new currency to control the financial turmoil on hand. However, the government based its anti-inflationary policies on an economic theory, believing that if the interest rate, cost, price, foreign exchange rate, and trade were all to be placed under tight control, then the market price would automatically go down by itself. Thus, the government failed to recognize the need to control the expansion of the money supply as well as the growth of the effective demands of the economy, in addition to the above-mentioned control measures. As a result, monetary reforms brought only a brief pause to the rising market price. Thereafter, prices resumed their upward trend. During the second half of 1949, prices rose 82 percent and another 34 percent in the first three months of 1950. Only then did the government realize the need to curb the island's wild expansion of money supplies and decide to use high bank interest rates to absorb the floating money in the economy.

In March 1950 the Bank of Taiwan announced a special savings program that offered an extraordinarily high interest rate—7 percent per month—which amounted to a 125 percent compounded annual interest rate. The high interest rate was specifically set to attract savings deposits against a background of an inflation which for the first three months of the year had been 34 percent. At a much faster pace than the government had expected, the public responded favorably to the high interest rate. Within a month, the total amount of deposits received in all the banks rose from 6 million new Taiwan (N.T.) dollars at the beginning of the month to 28 million N.T. dollars at the end of the month, which amounted to 7 percent of the total money supply. Most remarkable of all was that the inflation had thus been brought to a halt. When the savings program was announced, the inflation was running at 10.3 percent per month. However, during the first three months following the announcement, wholesale prices rose only 0.4 percent per month.

In July 1950, immediately after the outbreak of the Korean War, the United States resumed its economic aid to Taiwan. The aid brought, on the average, about U.S. $1.5 billion a year to Taiwan for the following fifteen years. During the same year, the United States and Taiwan signed a mutual defense treaty that committed the U.S. Seventh Fleet to patrol and secure the safety of the Formosa Straits. Expecting that these new developments would ensure Taiwanese confidence in the country's political stability and that the inflation would decrease as a result, the government authorized the Bank of Taiwan to reduce its interest rate on savings to 3.5 percent per month in July 1950 and another half point three months later. At the end of the year, total bank deposits dropped from 36 million N.T. dollars to 26 million N.T. dollars and the high inflation recurred. During the following year, inflation ran at an annual rate of 65 percent. Alarmed by the prospect of another bout of rampant inflation, the government authorized an immediate increase in the interst rate on bank savings, and once again the public responded favorably. The flow of savings into the banks resumed at a spectacular rate. By the end of March 1952, total bank savings deposits reached 271 million N.T. dollars, which amounted to 31.2 percent of the total money supply. A half year later, the total amount of savings had risen to 541 million N.T. dollars, which was 56.4 percent of the total money supply. Prices had become stabilized.

This success began Taiwan's long tradition of adjusting interest rates to control inflation. Owing to the absence of a money market, interest rates were determined primarily by estimations of the public's confidence in market price stability. However, this indicator had often set the interest rates too low, which usually caused the market price to rise again. Yet, whenever interest rates were raised again, prices always came down and bank deposits grew. Apart from using interest rates to control inflation, no other discernible principles were employed during this period to guide the nation's monetary or banking policies.

From 1950 to 1965, U.S. economic aid to Taiwan helped to pay off government deficits, financed major public utilities, transportation and communications projects, and formed a venture capital fund. Toward the end of the 1950s, Taiwan's inward-oriented economic growth produced an oversaturated market. The country now needed to develop export markets to relieve its overflowing domestic market. To facilitate this change, the government instituted new policies to effect export expansion. The Statute for the Encouragement of Business Investment attracted a large volume of foreign investments, a good portion of which came from the overseas Chinese. On the other hand, the high interest rate policy contributed to the accumulation of a large amount of savings which were used to finance the island's growing export industries. Together, these policies helped to form investment capital that made up the capital loss resulting from the termination of U.S. aid in 1965.

Foreign currency exchanges represented another area of monetary activities that was skillfully controlled by the government to maintain stability and to promote growth. In 1953 the exchange rate was set at N.T. $15.55 to U.S. $1.00; the rate remained in effect for seven years until it was replaced by a new rate in 1960. Under this rate, the Taiwanese currency was excessively overvalued. As a result, the overvalued currency hurt sales of Taiwanese products in the international market. During those years when the Taiwanese currency was overvalued and exports were adversely affected, in order to maintain balanced payments, Taiwan had to restrict imports through a strict import quota system and high import tariffs, and to limit outgoing foreign currencies through foreign exchange controls. Toward the end of the 1950s, when Taiwan was preparing to expand its exports, the overvalued currency was recognized as an obstacle to this effort. To remove this obstacle and still retain the prevailing foreign exchange rate, the government instituted a foreign exchange certificate, an official permit to obtain foreign exchange from the banks. Only the exporters were issued such certificates, which can be sold freely on the market at negotiable prices. By selling foreign exchange certificates to importers who were not eligible to obtain the certificate themselves from the government, the exporters were expected to make profits that would compensate for their losses incurred by the overvalued currency. The Bank of Taiwan exchanged at the official exchange rate of only 20 to 50 percent of the foreign currencies earned from exports and issued foreign exchange certificates for the remaining balance. However, starting in April 1958, the exporters were given foreign exchange certificates for the total amount of foreign currencies submitted for exchange. The selling and buying of foreign exchange certificates on the market set an actual exchange rate that was a lot higher than the official bank rate. In 1960 the government discontinued the certificate and adjusted the official bank exchange rate to the ongoing market rate, which was N.T. $40 to U.S. $1. This exchange rate remained in effect until 1973.

Because the exchange rate was pegged at N.T. $40 to U.S. $1, any extra foreign currencies brought into the economy through a trade surplus had to be absorbed by the Central Bank and the Bank of Taiwan through their foreign currency buying activities to avoid inflation. However, in 1960 Taiwan's exports began to grow until, in 1963 and 1964 its strong export performance greatly increased the Bank of Taiwan's net foreign assets. The increase amounted to a rise of 28 percent and 32 percent, respectively, of the total money supply. The disturbance to market price which this huge influx of foreign currencies could have caused was averted only by relaxing import restrictions to encourage spending on the international market. In 1964 the resultant increase of imports left Taiwan with a trade deficit of U.S. $66 million. In the 1970s a trade surplus once again produced a huge increase in the money supply—for example, 38 percent in 1972, 49 percent in 1973, 23 percent in 1976, 29 percent in 1977, and 34 percent in 1978. These increases unavoidably disturbed market prices in Taiwan. For example, the inflation rate of 1973 was an astonishing 40 percent. To counteract the force for inflation, the government raised interest rates to attract savings and in the meantime relaxed the control of capital flow to the international market and overseas tourist travels in order to absorb the inflated money supply.

Interestingly, this time, Taiwan had a foreign exchange problem quite different from the one it had experienced earlier. Instead of suffering from a foreign exchange shortage as it did in the 1940s and the early 1950s, the economy was troubled by an excessive influx of foreign currencies. The changed circumstance with respect to the foreign exchange supply in Taiwan naturally rendered obsolete the government's foreign exchange controls which had been in force since the 1940s for conserving foreign exchange reserves. Finally, in 1977 the fixed foreign exchange rate was abandoned, and the new Taiwan dollar was appreciated 5.65 percent to reflect its true market value. In 1979 a foreign exchange market was established in Taiwan, and the market's exchange rate was set daily by a joint decision of the Central Bank and five other major banks on the island. The adopted floating exchange rate enabled the economy to adjust to the fluctuating international trade performance, as well as to minimize the effect of imported inflation should it occur. However, some forms of foreign exchange control still remained—for instance, the eligibility to obtain foreign exchanges from the market was reserved for those who could provide proof that foreign currencies were needed for international business transactions. In 1987 the Central Bank withdrew all its influence on the exchange market. In 1988 all forms of foreign exchange control were removed; thenceforth, the government was determined to have a free money market. However, the government authorized the Central Bank to sell or purchase foreign currencies on the market to keep the value of the new Taiwan dollar at a desired level.[2]

Taiwan's stock market was established in 1962. Since then it has contributed to the formation of investment capital for the country's business and industry. To prevent trade irregularities on the market, in 1985 computers were installed to handle the trade. Since 1985, four investment companies have been permitted to bring foreign capital into the market. In 1974 Taiwan's money market was founded. Since then, the money market's interest rate has accurately reflected the supply and demand of capital in the economy. Regrettably, the small- and medium-sized businesses and industries have not grown accustomed to using the money market as a source of business capital.

Taiwan's financial system has evolved from its initial rudimentary form in 1949 to its current modern one. After China took over the island following World War II, the Nationalist government structured the financial institutes into a system, with the Bank of Taiwan functioning as the central bank responsible for executing the government's monetary policies and foreign exchange controls. In 1961 the Central Bank resumed its operations and took over the Bank of Taiwan's role as the nucleus of Taiwan's financial system. Since the mid-1960s, a number of specialized commercial banks have come into existence. The Farmers' Bank resumed its business in 1966 to handle agricultural loans. The Trust Bank was founded in 1971 to specialize in granting medium- and long-range capital loans to manufacturers. In 1974 the Trust Fund for Small- and Medium-Sized Businesses was established.

In 1975, in view of a wave of new banks coming into existence, the government promulgated a new banking law to define banking service areas and to set operational guidelines for each type of banking institutes. In 1976 the co-op savings institutes were consolidated to the Bank of Small- and Medium-Sized Businesses to specialize in business loans to small- and medium-sized businesses. In 1979 the Import and Export Bank was formed to handle medium- and long-term loans to manufacturers for machinery and equipment purchases. During the same year, the Transportation Bank was reorganized into the Development Bank to process loans for industrial development projects of "strategic" industries. The founding of the Development Bank was part of the government's effort to promote the development of capital- and technology-intensive industries in Taiwan. In addition, a group of co-op financial institutes and a number of commercial banks were formed. In 1972 the Agricultural Credit and Insurance Fund was established. In addition, the government encouraged the formation of venture capital funds. Some of the financial institutes drew their operational capital from savings deposits and others from special government funds. The variously specialized financial services provided by the banking institutes had pretty much addressed the banking needs of the island's businesses and industries. Since 1961, the growth rate of savings deposits has been at an average of 24.8 percent per year and the growth rate of business loans at an average of 22.5 percent per year. The government interpreted these figures as indications that its monetary policies were succeeding, which had been consistent in restraining public consumption while raising investment capital for the productive segment.

After 1958, a number of foreign banks set up offices in Taiwan. The First Bank of Japan was the first foreign bank opened to business in Taiwan, and there are currently more than thirty foreign banks on the island. (Thirteen of them are U.S. banks and ten European banks.) Nine other foreign banks only keep business offices in Taiwan. The ratio of business loans made by foreign banks to the total business loans granted to the island's businesses and industries increased from 4.4 percent in 1979 to 5.3 percent in 1986. The government passed legislation in 1986 permitting foreign banks to open multiple branches in Taiwan. This legislation also allowed a number of service areas to be operated by foreign banks. In 1987 trust funds and savings deposits were added to the list of permitted banking services operated by foreign banks. In the meantime, the entire financial system of the island was also expanded. In 1988 the government began to relax restrictions on opening brokerage firms, insurance companies, and banks. For instance, for the first time the insurance industry was opened to foreign ownership. In this way the government sought to remove obstacles to free operations of Taiwan's financial system.

In the last forty-one years the government has exercised skillful control over the country's fiscal system to facilitate economic growth. The government defined its policies on taxes and public spending as being (1) to effectively allocate resources, (2) to equalize the distribution of income, and (3) to ensure economic stability and growth. Nonetheless, the fiscal policies had different focal points at different periods of time. In the 1950s the emphasis was on raising government revenues and balancing government budgets, whereas in the 1960s the focus was on encouraging savings and investments through tax deduction incentives. The emphasis of the government's fiscal policies was switched from increasing government revenues, as in the 1950s, to cutting taxes to promote economic growth. Tax deductions for encouraging business investments did not result in reduced government revenues; instead, the revenues increased.

From 1950 to 1962, the government ran budget deficits that were caused primarily by high defense spending, costly refugee resettlement programs, postwar reconstruction projects, and low revenues. The deficits were covered by U.S. economic aid, bank loans, and government bonds. From 1964 to 1986 with the exception of 1982, the government enjoyed huge budgetary savings that were built on the enormously increased government revenues contributed by the fast growing economy. For example, in 1979 the government had a budgetary savings of 8 billion U.S. dollars, and in 1974 the savings totaled 6 billion U.S. dollars. A good part of the government's savings went to rural reconstruction, highway construction, defense arms, and subsidies to rice farmers. The annual average growth rate of government revenues during these years was 15.2 percent.

The major sources of government revenues were taxes, and income from government monopolies such as alcohol and tobacco sales and from government-owned industries and businesses. The major category of government spending was administration and defense, followed, in order, by education, science, culture, economic development, communications and transportation, and venture capital funds. The minor categories of spending have tended to gradually assume heavier weight in total government expenditures.

Since 1949, three major tax reforms have been instituted in Taiwan. In 1951 a unified tax collection law was passed requiring that all central and local taxes be collected by a unified tax collection system. In addition, a unified sales tax receipt was adopted to improve the effectiveness of sales tax collection. In 1955 the government launched an income tax reform to correct the lack of synchronization between itemized income tax collection and the collection of combined income taxes. All income taxes were consolidated into two categories: combined income tax and capital gains tax. The reform greatly increased the effectiveness of income tax collection. In fact, a year after the tax reform, government revenues doubled. In 1968 a government tax reform committee was established. During the following two years, the committee recommended that the bottom line of the lowest income tax rate be raised from 3 to 6 percent and the ceiling for the highest rate from 52 to 60 percent. Moreover, a value-added capital gains tax was proposed as a new income tax category. These recommendations later became law. In 1985 the newly established Economic Reform Committee (later, the Council on Economic Development) under the Executive Yuan made a number of proposals for fiscal reform. The committee called for an increase of government spending in public utilities and facilities and social welfare. Also recommended was a cut of income taxes to encourage business investments and higher participation by the workforce.

To implement a new business tax system that was aimed at reducing business taxes, the committee recommended that money supplies be reduced and that utility fees be kept stable, so that market prices would not rise after the tax cuts were made. In the area of tax collection administration, two major reforms took place. One was in the area of tax collection and the documentation of tax information. In 1988 the Center for Tax Information and Auditing was established, and a computer system was installed to process tax collection and auditing. Understandably, the computerized household registration immensely improved the collection of income taxes and inheritance taxes. The computerized tax system also stored and processed import and export duty deductions. A computerized database on government revenues and expenditures was also installed. The other reform involved the tax auditing system. An auditing system was set up to detect tax evasions and tax collection irregularities.

The ratio of government revenues to GNP in Taiwan rose from 1.6 percent in 1951 to 15.9 percent in 1986. Compared with the ratios of industrialized nations, between 20 and 30 percent, these figures are low. As a rule, the higher the weight of direct taxes in the total tax revenues, the more effective the tax system functions as a way of equalizing income distribution. In Taiwan's tax system, direct income taxes accounted for 30 percent of total tax revenues in 1953 and the percentage increased to 38.9 percent in 1986. In terms of the composition of the government tax revenues, before 1986 import taxes constituted the largest source of revenue, followed by commodity taxes. In the last few years, income taxes have become the largest source.[3]

The primary goal of Taiwan's fiscal policies was to promote economic growth. During the 1940s, faced with huge budget deficits, the government realized that only a rapidly growing economy could increase its revenues, which in turn could help balance the budget. In September 1960 the government promulgated the famous Statute for the Encouragement of Business Investments which offered tax reductions and encouraged savings to promote business investments and export expansion. Since its initial implementation in 1960, this piece of legislation has undergone a number of modifications. The statute expanded exports; increased savings and investments; and improved quality in research and development and rational management in industry.[4]

In 1955, in an effort to help expand exports, the government began to offer rebates on commodity, import, and defense taxes to export manufacturers. To encourage savings and business investments, a number of tax incentives were adopted. Beginning in 1985, the highest corporate tax rate was reduced from 30 to 25 percent. Qualified manufacturers were given either special tax deductions or depreciation deductions for a period of five to seven years. Downpayments for business investments were reduced, depending on individual cases, to a range between 5 and 20 percent. A tax exemption on 25 percent of taxable incomes was given to owners of manufacturing companies, large trading firms, and venture capital investment companies. Customs duties were exempted on machinery imported by qualified manufacturers. Investors who had kept stocks longer than three years were entitled to a tax deduction of 15 percent on capital gains. Interest up to U.S. $9,000 per year could be exempted from taxable income. Dividends earned from investments in brokerage firms that had tax deduction status were also deductible. To encourage research and development and rational management activities in corporations, a number of tax deduction measures were instituted. Research and development expenses were allowed to be deducted from taxable income. Equipment bought for research and development was entitled to tax depreciations. Patent royalties and incomes earned from innovative industrial activities were tax free. Income, stamp, and contract taxes incurred from company mergers were exempted.[5]

To promote export expansion, two separate import duty systems were established. One applied to countries to which the most favorable nation status was accorded and the other to those to which the privilege was not extended. The government was given the latitude to adjust import duties up to 50 percent upward or downward to changing domestic or international economic or supply conditions. In 1986 import duties were reduced across the board, and they were computed based on actual trading prices in order to be in synchronization with international practices.[6]

Taiwan's tax system was restructured to support the island's economic development orientation and energy-saving policies. Therefore, exemptions of commodity taxes were accorded to imported cotton and silk materials. Imported industrial materials were eligible for import tax deductions. High taxes were levied on products with high energy consumption.

The second important goal of Taiwan's fiscal policies was to maintain economic stability. In contemporary times, the stability of the economy had hinged on the government's ability to balance the budget. For a large part of its history, the national government ran budget deficits that usually led to money expansions and subsequent inflation. Since 1964, the increased government revenues along with the reduced government expenses enabled the government to maintain a balanced budget, which eliminated the need to expand money supplies and thus contributed to stable market prices. In the 1970s, facing an oil-related worldwide recession, the government increased its spending on public facilities such as highways, harbors, and electric power generation plants. During this time, these public construction projects singly kept the economy growing at 12.4 percent a year. This was frequently cited as an example of employing fiscal policies to counteract economic recession. Fiscal policies were also used to prevent imported inflation. Taiwan's export economy is extremely vulnerable to the inflationary impact of price fluctuations on the international market. Inflation in the country of its trading partners can easily be imported to its own economy if no preventive measures are taken. In 1971 the legislature gave the government the latitude to make adjustments on import duties up to 50 percent up or down, in order to offset major price fluctuations in the international market.

In 1973 a number of such adjustments were made on basic consumer products, industrial materials, machinery, and equipment. The adjustments eased pressures for price rises, thus minimizing the chances for inflation. During the oil crises of the 1970s, the government froze import duties on crude oil at its previous level in order to reduce inflation. To encourage industrial investments during the 1970s recession, the government re-enacted the duty reduction policy on imported machinery and equipment. In recent years, import duties have been reduced to encourage investments in manufacturing automation and environmental protection.

The government also sought to effect an equalized distribution of income. A combination of an incremental income tax system and increased government expenditures on education, health care, and welfare programs helped achieve equal income distribution. Taiwan's government officials were all too familiar with the fact that the outrageous income disparity between rich and poor in the old Chinese society had been a source of many social ills. Therefore, it was of particular importance that the government guard against a similar polarization of wealth on the island. Inheritance and gift taxes were added to the island's income tax system, and the income qualification level for tax deductions was progressively lifted. Qualifications for tax deductions on savings and stock dividends were lowered to N.T. $36,000 to benefit middle-income taxpayers. In addition, the government's expenditures on education, health care, and welfare programs rose steadily to bring income equalization benefits to low-income families.

NOTES

1. Both Executive Yuan, Council on Economic Development, *The Journey of the Modernization of Taiwan's Economy* (Taipei: Bureau of Economic Research, 1987), and Kwoh-Ting Li, *The Evolution of Policy Behind Taiwan's Development Success* (New

Haven, Conn.: Yale University Press, 1988), contain a detailed record of the government's monetary policies and the economy's reactions to these policies during the government's inflation-control efforts.

2. For further information on the history of the evolution of Taiwan's foreign exchange policies, see Executive Yuan, *The Journey of the Modernization of Taiwan's Economy*, and Li, *The Evolution of Policy Behind Taiwan's Development Success*.

3. For details on Taiwan's tax system, see Executive Yuan, *The Journey of the Modernization on Taiwan's Economy*, pp. 77–85.

4. Li, *The Evolution of Policy Behind Taiwan's Development Success*, pp. 138–139.

5. Executive Yuan, *The Journey of the Modernization of Taiwan's Economy*, p. 84.

6. Ibid., p. 85.

10 CONFUCIANISM AND THE CAPITALIST SPIRIT IN TAIWAN

Max Weber observed that there was a total absence of capitalism as an ideology in China. He attributed this lack to Confucianism. In his work, *The Religion of China*, Weber explained that Confucianism had created and perpetuated China's major social institutions and practices, all of which had stifling effects on the development of capitalism. Hence, Western-style capitalism had failed to emerge in China. He identified these social institutions and practices as (1) the patrimonial political structure and ideology; (2) an unyielding traditionalism in state affairs, which according to Weber, was reinforced by China's gigantic and cumbersome bureaucracy which was originally established to collect and allocate taxes; (3) the pacification attitude of the Chinese Empire and the resulting absence of wars in the empire; (4) the close-knit Chinese family sib and its constrictive effects on its members' freedom and creativity; and (5) the Chinese concept of the genteel as being a perfect product of Confucian education.[1] Over the years, Weber's study of capitalism in China has remained the authority on the subject. Weber asserted that the emergence of capitalism in Western culture was historically unique and owed its ideological origin to Protestant ethics as formed during the Reformation.

The causal relation which Weber so confidently postulated between the religious beliefs, culture, or value systems of a people—for example, the Protestant ethic in the West and the economic institutions in their society, such as Western capitalism—had a profound and lasting influence on later works in the field of economics and social sciences. One of the strongest attempts to expand the Weberian theory in the United States was based on the affirmation of the social institutions, in addition to the values and beliefs Weber identified, as an influence on the development of capitalism.[2] By negating the absoluteness of Protestant ethics as the determinant factor in the development of capitalism and by introducing the factor of social institutions, many scholars were able to explain the emergence of capitalism in societies where Protestant ethics had not been part of the culture.[3] Scholars who studied the history of capitalism in Japan had been confronted with a baffling question: while the Japanese and Chinese shared a cultural affinity, industrial capitalism emerged in Japan in the middle of the nineteenth century, but had failed to develop in China. Some scholars explained this paradox by pointing to differences in institutions and practices such as in property, political authority, occupation, social stratification, and kinship between these two cultures.[4] Other studies observed that the overseas Chinese enthusiastically engaged in highly competitive business endeavors; they attributed this very different phenomenon from what Weber had described about China, to the social environment of the host country.[5]

There is no widely accepted explanation for the apparent contradiction between Weber's view on the absence of capitalism in China and the obviously healthy capitalism seen in Taiwan. Both casual observers and international businesspeople who frequent the Far East have observed a similar work ethic, high energy level, and keen competitiveness among businesspeople in a number of Far Eastern industrial countries, notably Hong Kong, Japan, Korea, Singapore, and Taiwan, where Confucianism has had a profound influence on the local culture. The theory they espouse for the economic success of these countries is the very influence of the Confucian philosophy. The industrial capitalism operating in Taiwan appears to be no different from that which functions in the West and Japan. Taiwan's economy has even outstripped Western industrial economies in some respects. The entrepreneurial class that has gained power in Taiwan has markedly changed the power structure of that nation's politics as well as the perceptions and values in the society. Taiwan's capitalist economy, now rapidly maturing, has begun its march toward a full-fledged free market economy.

In light of all such developments certain questions concerning the origin of the capitalism currently operating in Taiwan have arisen. Did Confucianism contribute to the capitalistic spirit of Taiwanese entrepreneurs and businesspeople? If so, how can we reconcile this theory with the Weberian theory on the uniqueness of Protestant ethics as the cause of capitalism? If it is not the case, then what gave birth to the energetic industrial capitalist spirit of the Taiwanese? Assuming that Taiwanese capitalism had its origin in the Confucian cultural influence, then we need to explain how a religion or culture other than Protestantism could produce capitalism. Moreover, is there a difference in business practice between this and the Western branch of capitalism? We need to understand why Confucianism contributed to the emergence of capitalism in Taiwan but failed to do so centuries earlier in China when factors favorable to the birth of capitalism in the West were present in China. Two such factors were the discovery of a large amount of metal reserves and a rapid population increase in the sixteenth century.

In response to Weber's premise that Confucianism is the predominant religion in China just as Protestantism is in the West and Hinduism in India, Chinese scholars point out that Confucianism, though the prevailing influence in Chinese culture, is not a religion in the Western sense of the word. They state that precisely because of the overwhelming influence of Confucianism there was only a minimal need for a religion in China.[6] In fact, all religions transplanted to China more or less assimilated Confucianism into their belief and practice.

As recorded by his disciples, when Confucius formed his philosophy in the fifth century B.C., he refused to deal with the subjects central to religion—god, evil, salvation, and life after death. However, he did confer holy status on what he perceived as the metaphysical order of the nature which he variously called the world, nature, or heaven. He regarded it as the perfect paradigm to guide the operation of government as well as human affairs. He saw this holy order of the nature embodying a perfect state of harmony, and, being part of this order, he believed that society and the life of the individual should also be in harmony with this order. Therefore, people ought to seek harmony with the natural order through a life-long austere moral discipline in order to refine the spirit or inner self and elevate it to full union with the spirit of nature. Confucius believed that the perfect society must rely on orderly human relations; he identified these relations as those between the emperor and the state officials, a father and his sons, a husband and wife, between brothers, and between friends. For each relation, he specified responsibilities and privileges, and he established respectful and courteous rituals that the parties in the relation should strictly observe in order to preserve the social order. Certain ethical values and moral principles were to be followed in the pursuit of self-perfection. Confucius believed that ethical individuals had no need for man-made laws because they were self-guided by internalized moral principles. Instead, laws were established for the unscrupulous. Scholarly study of literary classics and the practice of ethical asceticism were recommended as the means to self-perfection. Confucius saw an intellectual understanding of the metaphysical order of the nature and the human society as a prerequisite to achieving moral superiority. This was the theoretical basis for the Chinese myth that a person's moral standards were commensurate with the level of education he or she had obtained.

In *The Religion of China*, Weber identified the social foundations and life orientation in traditional Confucian China that hindered the development of capitalism in that country. First, he pointed out that China's patrimonial political ideology and institutions had, in effect, prohibited the emergence of a bourgeois stratum whose class consciousness could open doors to the development of capitalism as did the capitalist class of sixteenth-century Europe.[7] Confucius envisioned the perfect social order, which was in harmony with, or a part of, nature, as having a patrimonial structure with the Chinese emperor, the son of heaven, as the head of state presiding over a huge, clearly stratified bureaucracy. Officials were expected to observe a set of elaborate ceremonial and behavioral rituals in relation to their respective superiors. These rituals were deliberately estabished to reinforce the social structure as well as the individuals' submission to tradition.

Within the patrimonial administrative structure, local officials were entrusted with certain patrimonial responsibilities; these responsibilities included ensuring that the people's basic sustenance was met, collecting taxes, maintaining dikes and roads, protecting the life of the people from the threats of bandits or rebellious uprisings, administering justice, and providing moral teachings and behavioral examples, an official responsibility unique to the Confucian tradition. The Chinese were taught to believe that the patrimonial political system was in perfect harmony with, or a part of, the natural order; therefore, its structure and existence were forever justified. The theological nature of the patrimonial administrative system demanded that the Confucian Chinese support the status quo. This line of belief had psychologically inhibited the Chinese from challenging the existing social order. Therefore, throughout Chinese history, open opposition to the existing social order had only been carried out by self-proclaimed rebels or secret societies. When dealing with the political powers embedded in the patrimonial social structure, the Chinese cajoled for favors and pleaded for leniency. There were no procedures built into the system for appeals, changes, or amendments. To organize people to gain political power would clearly be regarded as a rebellion against the existing social order, and thus against the emperor, and so would upset the harmony of nature. The concept of organizing people based on their common interests to negotiate for political powers, the kind of political and social struggles had led to the formation of a capitalist class in Western society, was therefore ideologically alien and repulsive to the Confucian Chinese.

Chinese emperors and their officials ruled not by constitutions but by their moral superiority. Public affairs were conducted based on the official's best judgments. The correctness of these judgments was ensured by the absolute ruling power of the highest ethical values and the selfless commitment to the public welfare—two superior moral attainments supposedly to be earned through an earnest study of the Chinese classics and an untiring pursuit of self-perfection. Law, in the Western sense of the word, did not exist in China; instead, the state administered substantive justice, a practice rooted in the very nature of the patrimonial Chinese state. Weber stated that Confucian China's unpredictable management of public affairs, which was usually legislated into laws in Western constitutional states, made capitalist endeavors extremely risky in China.

The patrimonial nature of the Confucian state also cultivated a peculiar practice that gave the local head official an unchecked power to collect and allocate taxes for the geographical area over which his office had jurisdiction. The chief official at each local administrative level, such as the provincial governor, the district head, or the city or village's chief officer was responsible for turning over to the official at the next higher administrative level a predetermined tax quota, so that the central government might be assured a certain amount of revenues. What was left from the collected taxes was the discretionary fund of the chief local official. Local officials often used these funds for staff salaries, social welfare programs, disaster relief, and bridge and road construction. Sometimes this fund was also a major source of the chief official's salary. The officials were often tempted to augment this fund through tax collection irregularities or open solicitations for contributions, fees, and gifts. Naturally, businesses became the prime target of tax irregularities and solicitations. The obvious vulnerability of Chinese businesses to abusive, precarious exaction of official and unofficial taxes discouraged capitalist endeavors. Modern social scientists trace the notorious absence of accurate bookkeeping to the tactics which the traditional Chinese developed to evade tax exactions. The office of the chief local official also had the power to exact corvée (civilian labor) for an unlimited period of time. Again, this practice could bring hardship to, or even devastate, the affected businesses.

Weber also pointed out an obvious lack of state leadership in China's economy. The production and profit side of the economy was left completely to the discretion of the Chinese people. Chinese imperial economic policy had merely been concerned with the financial aspect of the economy—fiscal and military finance.[8]

Weber identified the power of the sibs over the life of the Chinese as a major force inhibiting the development of capitalism in China.[9] A Chinese sib could consist of several hundred people related by blood and living in the same village. It had its own temple and school, set its own rules and regulations, and usually administered justice among its members. In dealing with outsiders, the sib rallied behind its members. A sib functioned as a social welfare unit that took care of its orphans, widows, and the feeble. The sib was also an economic unit, consisting of properties and incomes; expenses were shared among the members in much the same way as the members of a family do. An individual's financial assets were tied up with those of others in his sib. Under the circumstance, it became difficult to raise venture capital to start one's own business. Furthermore, an individual's education was usually paid by his sib; his obligation was to choose the occupation which the head or the elders of his sib had preferred for him.

Chinese sibs operated as self-sufficient economic units, which reduced the demands in the open market for consumer goods. As Weber explained, the trade guild in the Chinese city failed to form an organized power capable of bargaining with the city officials for protection and thus becoming the forerunner of a bourgeois stratum as did their counterparts in the sixteenth-century European city. The reason was that members of the Chinese guild had total loyalty to their sibs in the village, placing their wealth and hearts where their sibs were.[10]

Weber interpreted the literary education and the status-honor of the literati of the Confucian tradition as repressive to the development of a capitalist class in China.[11] The Confucian curriculum emphasized classical literature, political philosophy, ethics, history, poetry, and geography; mathematics, law, and natural science were excluded. Education was aimed at refining one's character, imparting ethical values, and cultivating the mind to aspire to high purposes in life. The occupational aspect of education was completely ignored. Confucius even expressed contempt for vocational education as being too narrow in approach and scope to be an education suitable for a gentleman. Crafts, trades, and engineering were regarded as work fit only for manual laborers. Profitmaking activities and other economic and financial aspects of life were considered to be too trivial and low a subject to concern the mind of a gentleman. The well-to-do family in the traditional Chinese society usually hired a financial manager to look after the family's wealth, its credit-lending activities, and the family-owned businesses. Stratification in the traditional Chinese society was based on occupation. The literati class was placed at the top of the hierarchy, followed by the farmers, laborers, and traders; in praising

literary learning and loathing profit-making, this structure reflected a
Confucian value. The literati was an honorable social class; its membership was not inherited but instead was earned through a person's achievement in literary study. Only the literati was qualified for positions in the
imperial bureaucracy or in teaching. In the Chinese view these occupations
required the use of intelligence as opposed to manual dexterity or muscle
strength. Wealthy merchants purchased imperial offices to become qualified for membership in the literati, and they encouraged their sons to
pursue a career that would lead to their membership. The Confucian value
system on occupation was repressive to the development of a bourgeois
stratum in China.

In spite of these institutional obstacles to the development of capitalism,
Confucianism imparted a set of ethical principles that were almost identi-
cal to that of the sixteenth-century Protestant—diligence, frugality, credit-
ability, honesty, rationalization, and self-control. The Confucian's moral
obligation to ascetic discipline was as strong and deep as the sixteenth-
century Protestant's sense of commitment to an inner worldly ascetic life
worthy of the saved persons. Although the Protestant heeded the call to
engage in a wordly profession with full dedication and commitment, the
Chinese intellectual submitted to the pursuit of becoming a "gentleman"—
a morally accomplished person who followed a high ethical standard. As
a result, the Protestant ethic produced the bourgeoisie in Europe; however,
the Confucian work ethic failed to do so in China. The failure apparently
stems from the negative value Confucianism accorded profitmaking. It
despised profitmaking as an activity involving greed, and deception. This
attitude gave the word "profitmaking," or "money" in the Chinese language a negative connotation. Confucius saw profitmaking as extremely
self-serving as opposed to what he regarded as an honorable endeavor: to
seek the welare of the masses. Money was regarded strictly as a means to
purchase the enjoyments of the flesh; wealth corrupted the spirit. Therefore, frugality was recommended as a way to guard against compromising
one's moral standards for material comforts.

Other than using money for credit lending, the Confucian Chinese had
no understanding that money should be made to generate the highest
possible profits. Chinese in the traditional society kept all their money and
valuables safe in the house and had no knowledge of the natural depreciation of the value or purchasing power of currency owing to normal
inflation. The ethical value which the early nineteenth-century English
philosophers, Jeremy Bentham and John Stuart Mill, saw in utilitarianism
was unknown to the Chinese. The Chinese did not see goodness inherent
in the creative use of capital for enhancing the economic welfare of oneself

or others. Therefore, Chinese merchants viewed their trade as merely a way to make a living. In fact, the archaic word in the Chinese language for commerce is "a form of making a living." They were usually apologetic about being greedy in their dealings. Certainly they did not see a fundamental goodness in using capital to stimulate the economy and to bring about improved economic welfare in the society—the very basic understanding that engaged Protestants of the sixteenth century in capitalist endeavors.

Clearly, then, the Chinese culture and institutions were antagonistic to the development of capitalism in China. Then, on what ground and how did capitalism develop in Taiwan? To answer this question, we need to consider the factor of change in the culture and institutions of China. The changing view of the Chinese about material wealth began about a century ago. During the second half of the nineteenth century, the repeated military defeats of the Chinese by the Western powers forced the Chinese to concede to the superiority of Western technology. Soon afterward, the Chinese engaged in a deliberate effort to adopt Western material culture and placed a high value on technology, science, and economic well-being. The treaties signed following these wars required that the Chinese open up port cities for international trade.

Chinese employees of foreign trading firms in these cities, by working alongside their foreign co-workers, learned Western business operations and acquired foreign language skills as well as knowledge of the Western way of life. To the Chinese, they represented a new class of businessmen. Many of them eventually set up their own businesses, often with business links with their former foreign employers. In addition, the Chinese government's modernization efforts called for establishing new industries in China such as armories, shipyards, mines, railroads, and communications. To prepare people to operate these industries, the Chinese government sent young, able officials overseas for technological, management, and business operations training. Employees of the foreign firm and the officials who had had overseas training became the teachers and pioneer practitioners of modern capitalism in China.

Even though capitalist thought and practice had thus been transplanted to China, the old institutions that had hindered the development of capitalism in China still prevailed. Sibs continued to be a constricting force. City trade and craft guilds has not yet become transformed into political groups to champion a bourgeois class in China. Government corruption and inefficiency continued to be a threat to business. Being politically and socially divided, China found it difficult to trade and transport goods between regions that were at war with each other. Multiple currencies, unfair and irregular taxes, and high inflation further increased the risk of operating a business in China. Most of all, political instability resulting from widespread, prolonged wars discouraged capitalist activities.

Certain major events of the nineteenth century changed Taiwan's general environment for capitalism. Fifty years of Japanese colonization had changed the island's cultural and institutional tradition. The patrimonial imperial Chinese authority was replaced by the Japanese colonial administration and its laws. Taiwan's secession from mainland China had further weakened its links to its sibs on the mainland. Certainly, Japanese businesses and industries had taught the Taiwanese intimate lessons about the capitalist spirit and had also tantalized their desires for economic success. Following the postwar repatriation of the Japanese, many former Taiwanese employees of Japanese businesses along with other interested Taiwanese took over some of the businesses and industries left behind. They became the first-generation capitalists of postwar Taiwan.

The relocated Nationalist government was committed to the development of the economy and, through the years, it implemented a series of social and economic reforms that created an institutional environment favorable to capitalism. The colonization experience had freed the island from the old Chinese tradition, and in addition the small size of the island had allowed easy program administration. Therefore, the Nationalist government's economic policies had a much better chance to succeed there than on the mainland. The constant threat of a Communist takeover consolidated government morale into an unusually high level of dedication and that was manifested in government employees' efforts to improve the economy. The government saw capitalism and entrepreneurial activities as two potent forces for the growth of the economy. They therefore planned to stimulate these forces.

This chain of developments in Taiwan's modern history helps us understand the shift toward capitalism. A question still remains to be answered, however: how was capitalism reconciled with Confucianism in Chinese culture? For capitalism, or any other body of thought, to influence the life of the Chinese, it had to be in harmony with Confucian philosophy. Capitalism found its way into the Chinese culture on Taiwan by appealing to Confucianism's heavy emphasis on the individual's achievements. In imperial China, the status of scholar-mandarin was a commendable achievement, which, in the eyes of the Chinese, brought glory and honor to the person's family. In postwar years, Taiwan's economic development won public support. This public support produced a change of attitude toward capitalist activities. The Taiwanese adopted business success as the modern goal of life just as the scholar-mandarin status had been intensely pursued in imperial China. Business success was sought in Taiwan with the same kind of singlemindedness, dedication, and family support as had been applied by the seeker of high office in imperial China. In addition, the government employed ideological indoctrination to urge the Taiwanese to exert themselves in business. Whereas filial obligations to familiy and loyalty to country were the two primary duties of the Confucian Chinese, in postwar Taiwan business success fulfilled both fundamental duties. Few Chinese can resist the call of his society to fulfill his duty as a citizen or a family member. It appears that the modern version of Confucianism in Taiwan actually motivated capitalism there.

Taiwanese businesspersons were also faithful practitioners of the Confucian virtue of diligence and perseverance. They commonly worked twelve or more hours a day, six days a week. The extreme competitive business environment required a high degree of perseverance to endure difficult times in business. The unreserved support of the family to entrepreneurial endeavors was an important factor behind Taiwan's economic success. A large proportion of businesses were family-owned and -operated. Often during the difficult early years, family members labored without compensation to help establish the business. Since commercial lending had not always been available in Taiwan, family members usually pulled their wealth together to support a budding family business. Again, the life-long, steadfast friendship which Confucius had defined as one of the fundamental human relationships played an important role in business life on Taiwan. In Chinese society friends, too, were expected to help each other in business. In fact, the Taiwanese tend to take friends along with family members as business partners, and, in times of difficulty, resourceful persons are expected to bail their troubled friend out.

On the negative side of Taiwan's foray into capitalism, the Taiwanese businessperson was inclined to pursue fast, immediately perceivable pecuniary gains. Companies were often short-sighted, and many of them, being opportunistic, were put together hastily, without the benefit of thorough business planning. Although extremely hard-work and fierce determination sometimes compensated for such shortcomings, the country experienced a high rate of business failures. This general business attitude may explain the lack of vision or goals in the business community for long-term progress. The absence of business leadership in this regard imposed on the government the responsibility to plan and initiate programs for economic growth.

It appears that the Confucian influence was also a barrier to rational business behavior. The Weberian definition of capitalism required that the accumulation of capital, the access to production means, and profitmaking activities all be rational behaviors—purposeful, goal-oriented, and effi-cient. However, the businessperson's decision-making ability was often burdened by a dependency on the traditions and conventions of the business community, and they might not be the most rational solutions to the business problems at hand. New business methods and approaches gain acceptance only when introduced and supported by government authori-ties. In addition, the average businessperson was unable to completely detach himself or herself from considerations other than the highest possible return of investment, the kind of rational decision making that Weber had said was characteristic of the capitalist. Heavy consideration was usually given to the preferences of familiy or friends in business decision making.

The limited scope of behavior covered in Confucian ethics appears to explain the present normlessness in Taiwanese behaviors concerning communal living. Confucius did not provide much guidance for behaviors beyond the realm of the Five Fundamental Human Relations which he identified and for which he established elaborated courtesy rituals to protect. To the casual observer, the extreme disorder of traffic on the streets and highways, the littering of public places, and the utter disregard for environment are the most notorious examples of the problem of normless-ness in Taiwan. Those business ethics prohibiting (1) counterfeited pro-ducts, (2) the reproduction of copyright-protected literature and computer software, and (3) the substitution of good product components with inferior ones, to the peril of consumer safety and health did not find any theoretical anchorage in Confucian philosophy. The Taiwanese had to borrow from Western thought to substantiate the moral imperative of these ethical principles, as they did for the issue of environmental protection.

NOTES

1. See Max Weber, *The Religion of China*, trans. Hans H. Gerth (Glencoe, Ill.: Free Press, 1951).

2. See William E. Halal, *The New Capitalism* (New York: Wiley, 1986).

3. See Norman Jacobs, *The Origin of Modern Capitalism and Eastern Asia* (Hong Kong: Oxford University Press, 1958), and S. N. Eisenstadt, ed., *The Protestant Ethic and Modernization* (New York: Basic Books, 1968), pp. 243–384.

4. See Jacobs, *The Origin of Modern Capitalism and Eastern Asia.*

5. See John Cornwall, *Modern Capitalism, Its Growth and Transformation* (New York: St. Martin's Press, 1977).

6. Yin-Shih Yu, *The Religious Ethics in China of the Last Centuries and Capitalism* (Taipei: Lienchien, 1987), pp. 41–94.

7. Weber, *The Religion of China*, pp. 13–32.

8. Ibid., pp. 50–54.

  9. Ibid., pp. 86–99.
 10. Ibid., pp. 95–99.
 11. Ibid., pp. 107–137.

11 ENTREPRENEURS AND THE SMALL- AND MEDIUM-SIZED ENTERPRISES

The entrepreneur's special role in economic development has long been affirmed by economists, though different explanations have been given as to what contributes to the making of the entrepreneur.[1] One thing the economists do agree on, however, is the entrepreneur's crucial role in setting up the chain of changes leading to economic development. Since 1949, entrepreneurship in Taiwan has been an important influence on the development process.

In a number of circumstances, entrepreneurship has made unique contributions to the economy. When the Nationalist government made its first effort to restore the economy, it relied heavily on the entrepreneur's ingenuity, industry, and willingness to take risk to revive the economy. Moreover, the vacuum left by the repatriation of the Japanese opened up unprecedented opportunities for economic activities.

The success of the agricultural redistribution placed large amounts of capital in the hands of the former landowners. As part of the economic development operations, the government encouraged and assisted the former landowners in investing the capital received from selling their lands. Many of them either obtained majority stock in formerly government-owned, successful enterprises, or they used the capital to establish new industrial enterprises. The success of the land reform policy greatly improved the farmers' economic condition; their demands for consumer products and farming machinery formed a strong market for the newly established industry. As a result, the dynamic product market in Taiwan further stimulated creative entrepreneurial activities.

In the turbulent aftermath of the end of Japanese colonial rule and the relocation of the Nationalist government to Taiwan, there were scant employment opportunities. However, economic restoration offered ample opportunities for entrepreneurial endeavors. In fact, the scarcity on the Taiwan market actually provided a favorable environment for these endeavors.

In the 1970s the government saw a need to accelerate the growth of industry and chose to rely on energetic entrepreneurialship to march Taiwan's industry into a new high tech era. Since the 1970s, the government has legislated a series of measures to encourage the high tech industry. The measures gave birth to a new group of high tech industry entrepreneurs, many of whom were scientists and engineers who had returned from overseas employment or businesses.

Entrepreneurial interest is widely held among the Taiwanese, and there is a high ratio of enterprises to population size. Amazingly, it appears that making money through entrepreneurial activities has been the islanders' favorite activity. The evident skewed emphasis of Taiwan's news media coverage on enterprising and financial activities further confirms this observation. Apparently, the country's unusually large number of small- and medium-sized businesses is the natural result of this widely held entrepreneurial interest. According to Ministry of Economic Affairs statistics, there are about 700,000 small- and medium-sized businesses in Taiwan. They constitute 98 percent of the total number of businesses, 65 percent of total export earnings, and 55 percent of GNP, and they employ 70 percent of the total workforce.[2] It is only natural, then, that entrepreneurial endeavors are widely attempted in Taiwan. Both ambitious young people, in search of worldly success in business, and retirees, in hopes of high returns from investing retirement funds and pensions, frequently enter into entrepreneurial arrangements. Abundant market opportunities resulted from the healthy economic growth, the government's industrial investment inducement policies, and the people's resourcefulness and ambition.

Any attempt to explain Taiwan's entrepreneurial drive must address the following two questions. First, is this drive a manifestation of the entrepreneur's charisma or a common expression of the modal personality of the Taiwanese society?[3] Second, how and what kind of innovations did the Taiwanese entrepreneur introduce to the economy?

To address these questions, a brief discussion of the emergence of Taiwanese entrepreneurs in the country's economic development is in order. There were no Taiwanese-owned major businesses or industries on Taiwan either at the end of Japanese colonization or four years later, when the Nationalist government resettled on the island. Modern Taiwanese entrepreneurs began to emerge after the relocation. In terms of the kind of challenges the entrepreneurs encountered in their own economic time, their biographical backgrounds, and the type of enterprises they were engaged in, Taiwanese entrepreneurs can be categorized in three groups: those of the early restoration period, those of the export-oriented growth period, and those of the high tech promotion period.

Most of the restoration entrepreneurs were former owners of large farmland who sold their land to the landless tillers under the government's land reform program. In return, as already noted, they received interest-bearing government bonds and stocks of government-owned enterprises. As part of the government's total economic development plan, capital received from land sales was to be channeled into industrial development. Therefore, with various incentive measures, the government was able to persuade the former landowners to invest in the island's industry. Among the basic consumer industries targeted for immediate development, fertilizer, textile, electrical power generation, and the cement industry were listed as top priorities.

The government continued to supervise the operation of the electrical power generation industry, and sold the Taiwan Cement Corporation, the major cement company in Taiwan, as well as the Taiwan Fertilizer Corporation, the major fertilizer company, to private individuals. As a result, the former landowners who held the majority share of stocks in these companies became instant entrepreneurs. Chen-Fu Koo, the current chairman of the board and president of the Taiwan Cement Corporation, was among this group of entrepreneurs. Koo considerably expanded his business, which currently includes a newly established electronics company. He also holds an important position in Taiwan's leading political party; he is a Central Standing Committee member of the Nationalist party (Kuomintang). At the same time, responding to the government's call for developing the textile industry, a group of wealthy families in Tainan, a major southern city and the imperial capital city prior to the Japanese colonization, set up textile mills along with those owned by textile industrialists who had relocated their business from Shanghai prior to the Communist takeover. During the restoration period, the government subsidized these industries with guaranteed government purchases and free technical and management consultations. It also set up strict import barriers to protect the industry's domestic market. At the time market supplies were scarce, the government heavily subsidized the industry, and market protection measures were effective. These enterprises had no choice but to succeed. However, this early group of entrepreneurs faced business risks and challenges unique for their time.

In hindsight, their decision to give up their land to become industrialists appears to be a wise one, but at the time when they were forced to sell their lands on which generations of their families had depended for a living, giving up the land meant a sudden loss of security and an uncertain future. These former landowners must have undergone a revolutionary change of attitude to trust in the government when it asked for their participation in building the island's industry and when it guaranteed to protect their economic interests during the transitional period. What is more, these former landowners had no prior training in operating the industry they now suddenly owned. Having been barred from any management responsibilities during the Japanese colonization, they may not even have had any notion about corporate management. In addition, then as today, industry depended on foreign sources for material and machinery supplies. These entrepreneurs suddenly found they had to learn to do business with international firms. Furthermore, under normal circumstances, inheriting a formerly government-owned industrial enterprise in Taiwan is no easy task, and when we add to this the private owner's novice status, the task becomes even harder. Traditionally, government-owned businesses in China were plagued with corruption and inefficiency and depended on guaranteed markets. The success of these new landowners turned entrepreneurs is a praiseworthy achievement.

The second group of entrepreneurs, those of the export-oriented period, appeared at the outset of the 1960s. The saturated domestic market, the availability of a large labor force, and the need for foreign currencies had driven the Taiwanese to phase out its inward-oriented economic growth and to begin an outward-directed approach emphasizing the development of labor-intensive, exported-oriented industries. As was true in many developing nations, industrial exports at the beginning of this period were primarily labor intensive, such as toys, plastic products, furniture, apparels, footwear, textile, and assembled electronic products. As the availability of inexpensive, quality labor in Taiwan became known to Western industrial nations, foreign contracts for manufacturing labor-intensive products started to pour into the island. As the demand for contracts mounted, experienced Taiwanese manufacturing workers began to set up shops to bid for them. Since labor-intensive manufacturing did not require complicated or expensive technology, shops set up by experienced manufacturing workers could easily handle the production contracts, especially when the contracting foreign firms provided product designs, production specifications, materials, and sometimes even technical assistance. These shop owners usually ran a very lean operation, and they were able to keep their bidding prices attractively low. Consequently, more foreign manufacturing contracts were drawn to the island, and more such shops were set up on the island as a result. A new group of Taiwanese industrial entrepreneurs had thus been born.

Since these manufacturing factories did not need to use advanced production technology or expensive machinery, the aspiring entrepreneurs of these factories did not need to be well educated or financially resourceful. Hence, the typical entrepreneurs within this group were former factory workers who eagerly grabbed the opportunity which the economy's export-oriented growth had suddenly provided. They borrowed capital, usually from relatives and friends, to finance their businesses. They took the challenge to learn all that was involved in operating and managing manufacturing enterprises, which included learning doing business with foreign firms. Because they dealt primarily with the contracted production orders of foreign firms, their businesses were sensitive to changing market demands in industrial nations, currency fluctuations in the world monetary market, and changing labor costs at home. Their businesses were often required to make major adjustments to changing demands and circumstances in the consumer markets of the industrial nations. Sometimes these adjustments meant a complete switch of product lines. Interestingly, during the turmoil of a sudden large-scale appreciation of the local currency, they came up with adjustment measures to withstand the shock of an abrupt and fast erosion of their competitiveness in labor cost, the comparative advantage on which they had built their businesses. The emergence of this new group of entrepreneurs represented a new route to upward mobility for a social class, the factory workers. This route had never before been available to this group. Therefore by becoming entrepreneurs they helped equalize income distribution on Taiwan.

The third group of entrepreneurs began to emerge at the beginning of the 1980s when Taiwan's economy took a leap forward into the high tech era. The government instituted many policy incentive measures to attract high tech industries. These measures included matching investment funds for returned overseas Chinese engineers and scientists who wished to establish high tech enterprises on the island. A generous tax holiday policy was applied to all high tech industrial establishments. Support services provided by the government ranged from a science park equipped with a complete line of facilities and amenities of a modern industrial park and an advanced research institute to support the research and development needs of the new high tech industry. Responding to the government's invitations, many overseas Chinese scientists and engineers, most of whom had resided in the United States, returned home to set up high tech enterprises in the technical area in which they had expertise. This group of entrepreneurs was young, highly educated, and inspired by the business success of Taiwan's prominent modern industrialists such as Yuan-Ching Wang of Formosa Plastics Inc. and those industrialists of Chinese descent in the United States such as the late Dr. An Wang of Wang Computers Inc. Their knowledge in science or engineering technology was the most valuable asset they brought to Taiwan's high tech industry.

To enable Taiwan's first-generation high tech industry to survive the keen competition coming from Japan, the United States, and other Western industrial nations, these entrepreneurs took high risks and met hard challenges. It is extremely difficult for a business to maintain a competitive edge in high tech fields in a land where research and development facilities, personnel, and funds are limited. As a new industry on Taiwan, the high tech industry did not have the benefit of the support of a network of suppliers and services. Moreover, these entrepreneurs had to compete in the world market with established, supersized international companies that possessed world class research and development as well as marketing and sales capability. However, the strong government support and assistance given to industry, the diligence and cooperation of the industry's employees, and, most of all, the hard work and ingenuity of the entrepreneurs may have given these enterprises an edge in the competition. In addition, the firm conviction and determination of these entrepreneurs to achieve the seemingly unachievable—"We too can produce the high tech products being put out by industrial nations"—may have played a part in creating a competitive high tech industry on the island.

Since 1949, entrepreneurship in Taiwan has exhibited a number of unique characteristics. First, major waves of entrepreneurial activities always followed the inauguration of new economic growth orientations. This might have to do with the commonly held belief of the Taiwanese that new business opportunities that result from the promotion of a new growth direction of the economy are particularly good for entrepreneurial endeavors because the government provides facilitating measures at the launching of a new economic orientation.

Second, the government played an important role in creating the above-mentioned three groups of Taiwanese entrepreneurs. Usually following the adoption of a new economic growth direction, the government instituted supporting policies to promote the adopted growth orientation and in the meantime informed the business community of the availability of the new business opportunities. With regard to the kind of innovations Schumpeter and Weber identified as being typical of an entrepreneur (changing the existing economic institutions and structure to form new patterns of business practices and activities), Taiwanese entrepreneurs apparently fell short of this definition. The Taiwanese entrepreneurs had traditionally looked up to the government for guidance in choosing their particular endeavor; this bred the entrepreneurs' habitual dependency and consequently retarded their creativity. This lack of creativity is seen in the peculiar phenomenon wherein entrepreneurial activities tend to congregate in particular lines of business that happen to be in vogue at a particular time. This phenomenon may also be attributed to the Taiwanese businesspeople's widely held belief that businesses are safe as long as they follow the lead of successful forerunners and are in synchronization with the business crowd. That Chinese culture demands conformity and discourages deviation may have perpetuated the dependency of the Taiwanese businesses on government.

Third, the family had traditionally been the basic economic unit in China, and this may have contributed to the unusually high proportion of family-owned businesses in Taiwan. While this type of enterprise offers plentiful advantages—a high degree of coordination and cooperation, solid financial support, and, in times of difficulty, family members pulling resources together to sustain the business—still, it forms a major obstacle to business growth and expansion. For the Chinese, selling family-owned properties for such sales is the most undesirable outcome next to declaring a bankruptcy. Because of the long tradition of holding onto family-owned properties, the Taiwanese owners are extremely reluctant to sell their family-owned business or enter a business merger. In addition, family-owned enterprises in Taiwan are notorious for failing to maintain auditable bookkeeping. As a consequence, they have difficulty obtaining bank loans. These practices restricted the family-owned businesses from taking advantage of modern forms of business financing.

Let us now turn to the two questions posed at the beginning of the chapter concerning entrepreneurship in Taiwan. Entrepreneurial spirit and interest are rather universally shared by most of the adult population on the island. It is more plausible that the Taiwanese entrepreneurship represents the modal personality of the island's capitalist culture than being a manifestation of a unique type of personality. When the relocated government, much reduced in size, could no longer offer the traditional route to success—the one leading to the scholar-mandarin—the favorable policy measures offered by the government as inducements to develop industry captured the Taiwanese's aspiration for achievement and made industrial entrepreneurship an alternative to personal success. Of course, the widely reported exemplary entrepreneurial successes reinforced the desirability of industrial entrepreneurship as a culturally approved route to personal achievement. Research recently conducted on the future career goal of Taiwanese junior high students indicates a pronounced shift from choosing the physical scientist, the category that had been most favored, to the industrial entrepreneur as an admired career.[4]

In addition to the innovations that each of the above three groups brought to Taiwan's economy, the entrepreneurs as a group contributed heavily to the flexibility, resilience, and adaptability of the economy. Taiwan's widely shared and extraordinarily active entrepreneurial spirit produced an overwhelmingly large number of small businesses. Because both the culture and the economy encourage entrepreneurship, it is only natural that the Taiwanese want to try their chances at becoming successful entrepreneurs. They either conscientiously run their businesses or diligently look for business opportunities. This kind of enterprising drive created an extremely competitive business environment in Taiwan.

The disproportionally large number of small- and medium-sized businesses in Taiwan became the backbone of the economy. Concerned for the island's social and economic stability, the government supported the continuing existence and growth of these businesses. The government recognized that since small- and medium-sized enterprises had been a widely favored route to economic success, they had contributed to the island's social stability and equalization of incomes, especially at a time when Taiwan was experiencing unprecedentedly high economic growth. It was also recognized that because this type of business had been in existence on the island for some time, they had assumed important functions. Widespread failure among these businesses could be devastating. Therefore, the government was committed to their stability and growth.

The fast changing manufacturing technology, the increasingly fierce international competition, and the growing complexity of the business environment on Taiwan presented hard challenges to these businesses, especially those that specialized in labor-intensive industries and had been operating strictly based on a competitive advantage in low labor costs. In light of these challenges, in 1981 the Small- and Medium-Sized Business Administration was established as part of the Ministry for Economic Affairs. The Administration was charged with identifying the common business difficulties of these businesses, and with referring them to consulting firms or service organizations for assistance. Over the years, the Administration developed sophisticated help strategies and diagnostic and consulting networks to upgrade the technology and management of these businesses. Early in its operations, the Administration pointed out that small- and medium-sized businesses commonly suffered from stringent capital, limited technological knowledge, and insufficient market information. The Administration therefore formulated the following help strategies: (1) to introduce the concept and practice of rational management and up-to-date production technology, (2) to assist applications for credit to finance new business ventures or to upgrade existing businesses, (3) to encourage business mergers or closer cooperation among businesses as a means of enhancing their competitiveness, and (4) to organize them into satellites of suppliers of materials and components of large corporations.[5]

The Administration formed three networks to deliver their diagnostic and consulting services. The first was a network to help the businesses obtain credits. Most of these businesses were operating with no financial plans, and the allocations of their company's financial resources usually followed no accounting principles. In fact, as a rule, they did not keep auditable books. This practice made it particularly difficult for the businesses to obtain credit from lending institutions. Banks in Taiwan normally required collateral for business loans. These businesses could not easily come up with sufficient credit to back up their loan applications. The major lending institution in this network was the Bank of the Small- and Medium-Sized Businesses, which worked closely with other commercial banks to process loan applications. The government also established the Trust Fund for Small- and Medium-Sized Businesses, expecting the administration of the fund to coordinate the services of a number of selected banks to provide credit guarantees to loan applications of these businesses. Businesses notified of loan application rejections were referred to the United Diagnostic Center for Loan Applications for free diagnoses and consultations.

The founders of small- and medium-sized businesses usually had limited technical knowledge and skills. With time, their technical inadequacies became a greater problem to the operation of their business. Their limited financial resources did not permit them to recruit technical specialists or to engage in extensive research and development activities. Thus, the Administration organized a second type of network to provide assistance and consultations in manufacturing technology and business management. The network consisted of the China Production Center, the Center for the Development of Metallurgical Industry, the Industrial Technology Research Institute, the China Textile Industry Research Center, the Food Industry Research Institute, and a number of private consulting firms.

Businesses may apply to the Small- and Medium-Sized Business Administration for assistance or consultation services on specific production or management problems. The Administration reviews the applications and then appoints consultants, chosen from the network's constituting organizations and firms, to take the assignments. Over the years, these businesses have applied for assistance mainly in the areas of manufacturing and material management, production facility improvement, and product upgrade.

The small- and medium-sized businesses were financially restricted from engaging in direct international marketing. They often relied on foreign trading firms to bring their products to foreign markets. The competition among themselves, as well as with companies in other Far Eastern countries, for the purchase orders of foreign trading firms was fierce. Often the price quotas they offered on their products contained only meager profits for themselves. Their products did not usually command steady sales or a customer market on which to build a stable business. The Administration established the third type of network to help these businesses develop alternative international marketing and sales tactics. The network consisted of all government and semigovernment foreign trade promotion organizations. These organizations collected and disseminated current international market information, and provided marketing and sales consultations and services.[6]

Taiwan's economy was particularly noted for its high entrepreneurial spirit and dynamic activities. These characteristics contributed to its ability to respond quickly to changes and opportunities in the international market. However, as pointed out earlier, the Taiwanese entrepreneurial spirit was founded on a striving for personal achievement which, in modern Taiwan, has come to be measured primarily in monetary terms. This change in value system took place following the island's great economic leap forward of the 1960s. Therefore, entrepreneurial activities have concentrated in those economic segments where large and fast profits are expected. At various times these segments have been labor-intensive manufacturing, import and export firms, real estate and construction, or, most recently, investments in the stock market. Time and time again, the oversaturated activities in certain areas have led to business failure. Their adverse effects on the economy are a source of concern to both government officials and economists.

NOTES

1. See Peter Kilby, "Hunting the Heffalump," in Peter Kilby, ed., *Entrepreneurship and Economic Development* (New York: Free Press, 1971), pp. 1–42.

2. *Small- and Medium-Sized Enterprises in Taiwan,* published by the Small- and Medium-Sized Business Administration, Ministry of Economic Affairs, Republic of China, 1988, p. 1.

3. See J. A. Schumpeter, *The Theory of Economic Development* (Cambridge, Mass.: Harvard University Press, 1934), pp. 62–94, and Thomas Cochran, *Explorations in Entrepreneurial History* (Summer 1965), pp. 25–37.

4. A 1989 Taiwan Normal University Research Report.

5. The *1989 Report of the Administration for Small- and Medium-Sized Businesses*, Ministry for Economic Affairs Press, pp. 4–8.

6. 1989 Task Priority List for Small- and Medium-Sized Business Administration, Ministry of Economic Affairs.

12 THE ROLE OF THE UNITED STATES AND JAPAN IN TAIWAN'S ECONOMIC DEVELOPMENT

International influence on national economies may take several different forms and produce several different effects. International economic development aids and loans as well as economic cooperative programs usually affect the receiving economy in a planned and structured manner. Through many other forms of contact with developing nations, however, industrially advanced nations may unwittingly influence the direction of the developing economy. Trade, capital investment, joint business ventures, exchanges of technical and management personnel, and economic advisers are among the common conduits through which the economy of the developing nation can be influenced by industrial nations.

International influences on developing economies may be visible in some less obvious ways. For example, rapid advancements in communication technology and the corresponding reductions of international communication costs have made new developments in science and technology in industrial nations almost immediately available to people in distant developing nations. The ideas and life-styles of economically advanced nations are also transmitted through the mass media. Certainly, visits and studies in industrially advanced countries have proven to be the ideal experience for assimilating knowledge and ideas. The transfer of knowledge, attitudes, and practices from foreign lands quietly, though persistently, molds and reorients the people of developing nations. International influences usually affect the developing nation's economic policies; capital, technology, and infrastructure; and economic institutions and human resources.

The United States and Japan have profoundly influenced Taiwan's economic development. Japanese influence came from Japan's fifty-year colonial rule and, later, the close trade relations between the two island nations. The friendship between the U.S. government and the Nationalist government made Taiwan open to U.S. influence which was chiefly in the form of economic aid from 1951 to 1965, and trade, personnel exchanges, economic advisers, business investments, and visiting student programs at U.S. universities. Taiwan's admiration for the U.S. democratic system as well as for U.S. technological know-how made the U.S. economy a natural model for Taiwan. On the other hand, Japan's postwar economic success has deeply inspired a desire for emulation in the Taiwanese.

The development of Taiwan's economy began immediately after the Japanese took over the island in 1895. The Japanese Empire invested heavily in Taiwan, which had now become part of Japan's repository of resources for economic and military expansion. For this mission, the colonial government drew up an ambitious development plan with a detailed implementation schedule. To this plan the Japanese applied their own successful development experience.

As its first step, the colonial administration inaugurated a series of land reforms. In 1896 it conducted a comprehensive land survey to establish an accurate tax base. This was the first such survey ever conducted on Taiwan, and the results became the foundation on which all later land registrations were built. The land reform policy demanded that the absentee landlords relinquich their land rights in exchange for interest-bearing bonds. In addition, land rentals were reduced to fixed rates. The farming incentives generated by the reform greatly increased agricultural production, which helped to transform agriculture from a tradition of planting merely for domestic consumption to producing for export markets. (Much later, the Chinese Nationalist government would apply these same reform tactics to its own land reform programs.) The colonial Japanese encouraged and helped the Taiwanese farmers establish farmers' associations as vehicles for disseminating agricultural technology and introducing new seeds and fertilizers. An extensive network of agricultural research centers and experiment stations was also set up for developing and testing new farming technologies. Later these colonial agricultural institutions and practices were utilized as major instruments of the Nationalist government's effort.

The second step in the colonial developmental strategy was to build infrastructure and human resources. Infrastructure built under this plan included the north-south railroad and highway system, postal and communications system, hydroelectric power plants, harbors, and flood control and irrigation systems. Human resources development efforts were concentrated primarily on the building of public schools, health clinics, and hospitals. Colonial developments laid down a solid foundation on which the Nationalist government would successfully build.

During its early stage, the Nationalist government faithfully followed the same development sequence established by the Japanese—obtaining technical assistance, increasing agricultural production, concentrating on labor-intensive industry with a low capital/output ratio, and stimulating trade export. Policy measures such as increasing productivity while holding consumption constant to accumulate savings appear to have been borrowed from the Japanese. Other examples of duplication were abundant during the export expansion period in Taiwan. Government officials in Taiwan commonly understood that similarities between the two cultures, as well as the fact that Taiwan's comparative trade advantages tended to be the same as those possessed earlier by the Japanese, called for a selective borrowing of policy measures from the Japanese experience. The pragmatism of Taiwanese government officials ensured a prudent borrowing of policies. The government had also borrowed a number of government organization models from the Japanese. For example, the China External Trade Development Council and the Bureau of Industrial Development were based on a Japanese model.

The Japanese influence on Taiwan's infrastructure is also evident. Decades later colonial Japanese investments helped promote the rapid growth of Taiwan's economy at the early stage of its development efforts. During the colonial period, the Japanese introduced a number of technological improvements to agriculture, including new seeds, multiple planting practices, and chemical fertilizers. Before World War II broke out, the Japanese brought agricultural and food processing industries and some manufacturing and heavy industries to Taiwan. These industries were selected based on Taiwan's designated supporting roles in the total economy of the Japanese Empire. When Taiwan rejoined China after the war, its political affiliation with Japan ended, but its previous colonial economic relationship was transformed into a close trade relation. For years therefter, Japan supplied most of Taiwan's imported goods and served as its leading export market.

When Taiwan's import market for Japanese manufacturing products grew to a certain size, the Taiwanese began to explore the feasibility of setting up their own manufacturing plants to replace imports. To access the needed technologies, they often invited the Japanese producers of the import goods to become partners of their new business ventures. This kind of business cooperation built up the island's bicycle, motorcycle, house appliances, and industrial components and materials industries. On the other hand, when labor costs at home became excessive to Japanese producers, they first considered moving operations to Taiwan to take advantage of the island's competitive labor cost and convenient location. The Taiwanese, aware of the advantages they provided, maximized the technological advancement of their own industry. The Japanese also sold equipment and machinery and provided technical consultations to the Taiwanese. Certainly, the close geographical location between the two countries allowed rapid transmission of Japan's latest technologies.

Among colonial Japan's most important legacies were its economic institutions and values. The agricultural institutions established during the period—especially the farmers' association, agricultural research centers and experiment stations, and credit unions—have all become integral parts of today's agriculture. The Nationalist government inherited the colonial apparatus of government monopoly, including the Food Bureau, the Bureau of Tobacco and Alcohol, and a banking and marketing system. The colonial Japanese also left a tradition of hard work and discipline, and instilled in the Taiwanese a receptivity to changes and an appetite for technological progress. To the Taiwanese, Japan represented the successful modern Asian nation. Colonial Japan's vigorous economic efforts inspired admiration among the Taiwanese. The Taiwanese as consumers witnessed the operation of modern business, which prepared them psychologically for the advantageous economic opportunity that opened up after Japanese businesses left.

The Taiwanese, angered by Japan's wartime atrocities in China, did not readily acknowledge the Japanese role in their economic development. Nonetheless, being pragmatic people, they took full advantage of business cooperation opportunities with their former foe. Taiwan's concern for its trade deficits with the Japanese and their wariness of the so-called economic invasion of the Japanese led them to push their products into the Japanese market. Despite all their cautions against their possible dependency on the Japanese economy, the close economic relationship that has existed between the two nations for nearly one hundred years is not easily reversible. Taiwan's recent efforts to increase trade with countries other than Japan and the United States have markedly reduced its dependency on these two markets. Nevertheless, Taiwan will likely continue to regard Japan as a source of technology transfer, as a major export market for its products, and, most of all, as a model of economic growth and technological progress.

The long-standing friendship between the Chinese and the United States facilitated the United States' ability to influence the Chinese government.

This friendship originated in the nineteenth century during a tumultuous period of China's foreign relations with Western powers after the Opium War. Following the Opium War, with China in peril of having its territory divided as colonies of the major world powers, the United States came to its rescue by proposing an open door policy. China, it was proposed, would be open to trade with all world powers, thereby obliterating the need to parcel out the vast Chinese kingdom. The Chinese deeply appreciated the U.S. help and was determined to pay back with a loyal friendship. During the entire Nationalist rule of mainland China, American advisers played an important role in the government's policymaking. The U.S. advisory role in China expanded rapidly during World War II when the two countries engaged in extensive military cooperation in Asia. Through their wartime cooperation, many Chinese government officials formed close friendships with their U.S. advisers and U.S. government officials. These friendships later became a major conduit for U.S. influence on Nationalist China.

When the Korean War broke out, Taiwan became an important strategic point in the U.S. security defense of the Pacific Basin. In 1950 the United States resumed its economic aid to Taiwan, strengthening its military capability and economic stability. For the next fifteen years, the United States poured about $1.5 billion of aid into Taiwan, averaging about $10 dollars a year for each person on the island. In 1953, the third year of U.S. economic aid to Taiwan, the Mutual Security Agency (MSA), the aid-granting organization, listed three goals of the aid in its report to the U.S. Congress. First, it sought to maintain the economic stability of the island. MSA recognized that Taiwan's control of its rampant inflation was pre-requisite to progress in other areas, as well as to balancing the budget and effecting orderly financial operations. The second goal was to support the U.S. military effort, which was carried out in three ways: (1) providing counterpart financing of local projects recommended by the Military Assistance Advisory Group such as airfields, barracks, harbors, and ware-houses; (2) furnishing counterpart funds to cover government budget deficits arising from high military spending; and (3) finishing the construction of joint-use facilities, such as highway bridges, harbors, railways, and power plants. The third goal was to improve Taiwan's capacity for self-support.[1] MSA's policy was to make possible the reduction or termination of aid through planned development. During the first three years of aid, MSA's principal effort was to rehabilitate outdated or undermaintained plants; assistance was planned for expanding existing plants and building new plants where the markets warranted.

At each five-year interval of the total fifteen-year aid period, a change of direction in aid assistance occurred. From 1951 to 1955, the assistance concentrated on promoting economic and political stability. Taiwan's economic condition in 1951, the year the aid began, was deplorable. A widespread shortage of food, clothing, and other basic necessities threatened the country's political stability. Heavy military defense expenses had created huge budget deficits. The out-of-control inflation was much like the inflation that had caused the Nationalist government to lose the mainland a few years earlier. Three years of injecting large amounts of aid into Taiwan effectively curbed the inflation and sharply increased real per capital income. In July 1954 the Chinese Communist assault on Quemoy was repulsed; Taiwan had demonstrated its defense capability. In 1955 the United States and the Nationalist government signed the Treaty of Mutual Defense which committed the two countries to a long and stable relationship.

From 1956 to 1960, the objective of U.S. assisitance shifted from military strength and monetary stability to economic development. This aid objective was never made explicit. It was carried out as an integral part of the defense support of Taiwan because it was feared that the U.S. Congress would find it harder to vote for an aid package aimed at economic development of a friendly nation than one aimed at defense support. During this period, U.S. aid advisers worked with the Chinese government to improve and refine programs for achieving a self-supporting economy. Joint-approved development plans were drawn up based on an agreement on the armed forces level and the civilian consumption standard. The U.S. aid package made a heavy commitment to infrastructure and industrial projects. In 1959 loans for capital projects were first made to Taiwan. Rapid development occurred during this period. Real GNP per capita rose by 0.4 percent in 1956, 3.7 percent in 1957, 3.2 percent in 1958, 4 percent in 1959, and 4.4 percent in 1960.

In 1961 U.S. assistance to Taiwan was given a new goal: reduced emphasis on general economic development and increased concentration on nurturing private enterprise, promoting exports, and terminating U.S. concessional assistance. This shift was the product of a new view in the U.S. Congress regarding the goals of American assistance programs. Now the thinking was that economic social development should be a high-priority of U.S. foreign aid programs and the development of private enterprises should be emphasized. The founding of the Industrial Development Investment Center and the China Development Corporation in 1959 reflected this new emphasis. In the same year, U.S. aid officials recommended that the Chinese government adopt a comprehensive set of policies to encourage private investment and export. In 1960 the Chinese government promulgated the famous nineteen-point Program of Fiscal and Economic Reform. This program improved the investment climate on the island, and, as a result, exports rose rapidly. In 1965 U.S. aid to Taiwan came to an end. The United States had helped Taiwan establish its creditworthiness with World Bank and other international financial institutions and gain technical assistance from U.N. and other international and U.S. agencies. Therefore, with the end of U.S. aid, Taiwan actually broadened its international source of economic assistance.[2]

The termination of U.S. aid marked the end of planned and organized U.S. influence on Taiwan's economic development. Yet Taiwan's new externally oriented economic growth direction begun during the 1960s unwittingly subjected its economy to U.S. influence in an even greater measure. Taiwan's trade with the United States grew rapidly after 1960, and in the early 1980s, in volume traded Taiwan had become the United States' fourth largest trading partner. In the last forty-one years, the United States and Japan have had the largest share of Taiwan's annual imports. U.S. influence on Taiwan's economy after U.S. aid ended occurred through three channels: technology transfer, trade, and visiting U.S. consultants to the Chinese government.

As discussed in Chapter 7, the birth of Taiwan's electronic industry was linked to technologies brought in by the local plants of American-owned electronics companies, such as General Instruments. American businesses that had contracted with Taiwanese manufacturers also played an important role in introducing U.S. technologies to Taiwan. Taiwanese dealers of American products as well as Taiwanese engineers and scientists who had returned from the United States were able agents of technological transfer.

Through the years, the extremely enterprising Taiwanese amply demonstrated their ability to turn newly acquired technology into successful products. An interesting series of reactions occurred each time a new line of industry was introduced to Taiwan: a backward chain of suppliers of materials and parts to the new industry would first come into being; a few years later, ambitious experienced engineers in the new industry would quit their jobs to start their own businesses which would now be in competition with their former employers; and the rapid development of the businesses of the suppliers and the new industry itself would necessitate the rapid expansion of the export market. The Taiwanese goal to elevate their country to the status of an industrial nation required rapid technological advancement. Therefore, they earnestly sought after the transfer of new technologies. Beginning in the 1960s, following the promulgation of the reform policy to encourage foreign investments, there was a steady flow of U.S. companies to Taiwan to establish manufacturing plants. As expected, these companies made vast contributions to Taiwan's advancing technology. Since the 1960s, the United States has been the largest export market of Taiwanese products; therefore, Taiwanese industry orients its products to U.S. demand.

The Nationalist government regularly invites U.S. economic consultants to visit Taiwan and to give advice on important economic issues. In recent years, nearly every Nobel laureate in economics has been invited to Taiwan to share their wisdom on solutions to the island's economic problems. Their analyses are studied, and their recommendations are faithfully followed.

The United States has also had an immense influence on Taiwan's human resource and economic institutions. Taiwan's admiration of U.S. democracy and technology has made the United States a natural model for its technological and economic advancement. Taiwanese students often choose to do their graduate work in the United States. For years, the Taiwanese have constituted the largest foreign student body in U.S. universities. In addition, every year the government sends a large number of engineers, scientists, and military personnel, to the United States for study and training. American textbooks are commonly used in universities and colleges in Taiwan, and Taiwanese elementary and secondary educators have regularly been sent to the United States to study curriculum design and instructional methods. On the other hand, through frequent business contacts with Americans, the Taiwanese have assimilated U.S. business and marketing practices. Years of U.S. advice to depoliticize the economy and to allow free market functioning are beginning to have their effect.

The Taiwanese, having worked long and hard to develop their economy, are understandably reluctant to acknowledge the help of any foreign country in their economic success. Yet, the debt is there. A closed and static society such as ruled Taiwan was simply not capable of generating the seed of its own changes.

U.S. influence on Taiwan's economy has gone beyond the face value of the $1.5 billion the United States delivered between 1951 and 1965. For example, the aid money eliminated the need for the government to continue its desperate inflationary practice of printing money and thus stabilized the island's finance. On the other hand, the U.S. decision to aid Taiwan itself communicated to both the war-wary Taiwanese and prospective foreign investors the United States' strong commitment to the island's security at a time when Taiwan's questionable political status had discouraged investors.

The strong military assistance component of the U.S. aid package relieved the Nationalist government of its heavy burden of military spending and allowed the government to commit more of its resources to economic development. When the Mutual Defense Treaty was signed in

1953, and the U.S. Seventh Fleet was consequently assigned to patrol the Formosa Straits, Nationalist government officials began to breathe a sigh of relief, and economic development started to take on greater meaning for the otherwise preoccupied officials.

The benefits of economic policies and programs jointly developed by the aid advisers and the Nationalist government officials went beyond their substantive values. In the process of cooperation, the Taiwanese were exposed to modern planning concepts and techniques, as well as to the real-life experiences of putting capitalist principles into practice through economic policies and planning. This learning experience was beneficial to economic modernization. The officials were also introduced to the desirability of the market economy.

U.S. aid had yet more secondary benefits. The government adopted the U.S. recommendation to develop the private sector and to promote foreign trade. These new policies turned out to be a timely strategic move that put the island on its way to remarkable economic growth. When U.S. aid ended, the United States also recommended Taiwan to international economic development and cooperation organizations as well as to economic assistance agencies in the United States; the Taiwanese have wisely used these resources to further their development. Finally, the United States has been the major export market of Taiwanese products, and Taiwan's economy has been heavily dependent on its foreign trade performance. This has made the U.S. market an important determining factor in Taiwan's economy.

The United States now has huge trade deficits with countries like Japan, Korea, and Taiwan—the very countries whose economy the United States helped develop. Is there a connection between the U.S. development strategy for foreign economies of decades ago and the current U.S. trade deficits with these countries? Did the United States, through its aid programs, form an economic relationship with these countries that inevitably led to the dependency of these countries' economies on the U.S. market and the subsequent U.S. trade deficits with them? Should U.S. economic aid programs to developing nations conscientiously help the recipient country avoid developing an economy with a heavy dependency on the U.S. market? The primary goal of U.S. economic aid to these countries was to secure their political stability and to lift the respective economies out of conditions that made them susceptible to Communist powers.

When Taiwan's economy took off, it unmistakably headed toward exports with a heavy dependency on the U.S. market. By the early 1960s, U.S. aid advisers and the Nationalist government had jointly decided to steer Taiwan to a export-oriented growth by promoting the labor-intensive export industry. The logic behind this strategy was that the island's low-cost labor would give the industry a competitive edge in the high labor cost U.S. market. As a result of this economic development effort, the textile, apparel, footwear, sporting goods, machine tool, and furniture industries were established on Taiwan. These were the very industries to which the United States had, in the last few years, applied restrictive import quotas in an attempt to reduce its trade deficits with Taiwan. When the development of labor-intensive industry was proposed as a growth strategy for Taiwan's economy, U.S. aid advisers also recommended that the island's consumption be maintained at a steady level so that savings could accrue. One policy measure adopted to curb the country's consumption level was to discourage the import of luxury items by levying a heavy customs duty on these items. For some time, the luxury item category encompassed almost everything other than industrial equipment and materials. The ultimate consequence of promoting exports to the United States and setting barriers on importing luxury items was a trade surplus in Taiwan's economy.

Taiwan's economic growth is locked into a pattern of heavy dependency on the U.S. market, and it is extremely difficult to break out of this fixed mode of international trade. Decades of close business ties with the United States have made English the second language on the island, the United States the most studied export market of Taiwanese businesses, and U.S. manufacturing standards and specifications the production guides of Taiwanese manufacturers. Moreover, an elaborate chain of demand and supply has developed between the two economies. In recent years, in an attempt to balance trade with Taiwan, the United States has exerted pressure to appreciate the value of the island's currency and has called for voluntary control of exports to the United States. Taiwanese compliance with this request resulted in a deep industrial recession, idled capital and labor, and high inflation, even though the sudden 40 percent increase in the people's wealth owing to the currency appreciation offset some of these financial losses. The remarkable resilience and flexibility of Taiwanese businesses enabled them to adjust swiftly to the resulting turbulent changes. By heavily investing in businesses abroad and relocating labor-intensive industry overseas, the Taiwanese took advantage of the steep appreciation of their currency in the international market and at the same time circumvented the new U.S. trade restrictions.

This ability to adjust should not be counted on at all times. While the unusual degree of solidarity among the Taiwanese people and the flexibility of their economy have enabled them in the past to avoid paying too high a social price, failure in the test of economic adjustability could devastate the economy. To steer developing economies such as Tiawan's from dependence on the U.S. market and, in the meantime, to encourage a balanced growth of these economies' export markets would not only prevent the United States from running too big a trade deficit with the nation, but would also strengthen U.S. leadership in world economy.

NOTES

1. Neil Herman Jacob, *U.S. Aid to Taiwan* (New York: Praeger, 1967), p. 31.
2. Ibid., pp. 227–237.

13 WHERE TO GO FROM HERE

Our examination of Taiwan's rise to economic power in this book was heavily influenced by the economic development theory of Simon Kuznets. In this theory, Kuznets explains that a small number of countries, including the so-called newly industrialized countries of Taiwan, Korea, Hong Kong, and Singapore, entered an era of modern economic growth after World War II through technological innovation in production, and made the social and institutional changes that facilitated a continuing increase in per capita or per worker product. Thus, Kuznets views these countries' succession to modern economic growth as a function of their readiness to systematically apply existing scientific and technological knowledge to production. Their high rate of growth in per capita and per worker product was accompanied by rapid shifts in production and social structure, which are usually referred to as industrialization, urbanization, movement of the labor force to employee status, and the like. Kuznets underscores the importance of the national government in organizing the human element for realizing economic growth potential.[1]

Specifically, Kuznets' theory influenced the structure of this book in the following ways: the book's international and historical dimension, its focus on the dynamic interplay between institutional changes and economic growth, and its attention to government policies. In earlier chapters we discussed the dramatic beginning of China's journey into modernity: its awakening to the economic value of sciences and technology and its subsequent determination to apply that knowledge to construct the economy. During the mid-nineteenth century, the European and U.S. expansion in Asia forced self-contained, isolated China to open up to foreign trade and Western influence. The unequal treaties that the Western military might force on China shortly thereafter shocked the Chinese into the realization of the power of Western technology, and thus they were faced with the urgent need to rebuild their nation through modernization. Charged with a high degree of nationalism, the Chinese engaged in an ambitious program to transform their nation into a modern industrial democracy modeled after the Western nations. In the effort, the Chinese embraced Western technology, science, and democracy and many other Western concepts and values while subjecting their traditions and institutions to critical evaluations. Thus began a century of massive, sometimes violent, cultural and institutional changes in China which only a century later made it possible for Taiwan to experience modern economic growth.

This one hundred-year span in China was filled with war and turmoil. Actually, it is difficult to determine whether the social or institutional changes necessary to effect China's modernization had caused the war and turmoil, or whether they inevitably brought about the desired social or institutional changes in that country. Foreign economists and observers, seeing this enormous land wasted in a series of civil wars, the huge population besieged by poverty and imprisoned by tradition, and the ponderous Chinese bureaucracy plagued with incurable corruption and inefficiency, pronounced the country a hopeless case for economic development. As shown in earlier chapters, the relocation of the Nationalist government to Taiwan suddenly presented the Chinese people in Taiwan with the most favorable condition ever to enter into modern economic growth. Well-designed, pragmatic programs were launched, but without the people's determination to survive Communist threats and to prosper economically the new economic policies and programs would never have succeeded. Step by step, from postwar restoration to import substitution, to export-oriented growth, to promotion of heavy and chemical industry, to the current high tech stage, Taiwan's economy has stayed on a continuous growth pattern.

Development economists like Kuznets have dealt extensively with structural prerequisites to modern economic growth. Their theories explain that the presence of certain structures has enabled the economies to break out of long-standing stagnation or slow growth into an era of rapid, steady growth. Yet, these economists provide little account of the structural changes that took place after the economies entered modern economic growth to ensure steady growth. Since the 1960s, rapid, dynamic changes in Taiwan's economy have allowed its steady growth to continue. This chapter attempts to identify the major trends in structural changes that will likely continue into the future, with the hope of making some predictions about the future state of the economy.

Both the Nationalist government's proclaimed intents and its latest actions suggest that a trend of change is in the making. The government is seeking to liberalize the economy, that is, to institute a policy of noninterference.

From the onset of its modernization a century ago, China's government played a central role in initiating technology transfer, cultural change, and social reform, building infrastructure, national defense, and human resources, instituting modern financial and communications systems, and championing the development of new industries. The government's central role in China's modernization was a result of both the practical needs of the time and the influence of its founding father, Dr. Sun Yat-Sen. Centuries of the scholar-official tradition in China had concentrated the best minds and talents in the national government. Moreover, government officials tended to have the greatest access to Western knowledge and consultants. At that time, modernization was equated with Westernization; therefore, Western-educated government officials became the natural leaders of China's modernization.

The state of the economy in China did not permit its private sector to have the resources it needed to shoulder its share of responsibilities in modernization. Therefore, economic realities demanded that the government assume the central role. In his Three Principles for the People, Dr. Sun Yat-Sen, fearing private monopoly of those industries affecting the supply of basic necessities, called for state ownership of industry. Later, the Chinese Nationalist government faithfully incorporated this instruction into its constitution.

The government's leadership role continued after the National government moved to Taiwan. After the war, the government inherited the major industries and businesses from the departed Japanese. Although some of them were later transferred to private ownership, the government still kept most of them under its control. Then, in the 1970s, as part of the government's effort to promote heavy and chemical industries, it set up steel, petrochemical, and nuclear energy industries which significantly increased the proportion of government-owned enterprises. In addition to owning a large number of enterprises, the government now assumed primary responsibility in planning economic development and led its entire economic development effort. In addition, taxes, foreign exchange rates, and import duties were frequently manipulated to encourage investments or to control imports, exports, and market prices. Undeniably, the government had a decisive role in Taiwan's economy.

From the beginning of Taiwan's economic development, the government systematically nurtured the private sector and coaxed it into playing important roles in economic development. As the private sector grew, the vigor of its enterprises set off a natural growth mechanism in the economy in which the industrial section began to thrive in a robust backward and forward chain expansion and the service industry started to take off. The greatly increased size and strength of Taiwan's private enterprises gave them the confidence to demand that the government interfere less in the economy—a sign of the economy's coming of age. Taiwan's self-imposed pressure to speed up technological and industrial growth made it impatient with the natural pace of its economy, and the demand arose for an economic leap forward. From time to time the government introduced new technologies in industries to accelerate growth. A typical example is the government's promotion of eight strategic industries in the mid-1980s. Recent changes involve the government's withdrawal of its influence from the financial market and the reduction of state-owned enterprises, government subsidies, and import controls. These changes have all been aimed at facilitating a completely free market economy on the island. Nevertheless, in its determination to liberalize the economy, the government appears to be unlikely, in the near future at least, to give up its strong leadership in the high tech industries.

When the economic growth of a developing nation is guided by capitalist principles, then the progress of the development forces changes in the nation's social structure and institutions to allow the free operation of the principles. Apparently, this kind of change has been taking place in Taiwan in two separate cultural and behavioral areas. First, as the guiding principle of business decision making, a strict cost-effectiveness calculation has begun to replace all nonrational factors, such as loyalty to family, which before had occupied important places in Taiwan's business. In this regard, the Taiwanese have come a long way: from a tradition of running businesses partially to provide employment for and to distribute welfare to extended family members to operating them as rational, profit-oriented organizations. Since business decisions based on factors other than cost-effectiveness are counterproductive to capitalist goals, it is imperative to free business behaviors from the bondage of this tradition and return economic activities to the rule of capitalist principles. There is clear evidence of a movement toward rationalization of business activities in Taiwan: an increasing number of businesses now engage in merit-based hiring and promotion practices; and the board of directors, rather than the owner's relatives, control major business decisions (though some board members may be related to the corporation's founding family). The practical minded Taiwanese are expected to continue making progress in this regard.

The second area of change involves the emergence of community consciousness in economic activities, which was notably missing during Taiwan's early economic development. Capitalist business behavior is motivated by the belief that business profits represent a measurable achievement of one's discipline and that economic production and its related activities should serve the common good. Therefore, economic activities should entail an element of service. In contrast, the individual achievement-oriented Confucian tradition regards the business world as a modern field of competition testing the player's ingenuity and industry. Success in business brings glory to one's family.

Beginning with the export expansion period, a nationalistic sentiment became attached to business activities in Taiwan; good performance on the international market was regarded as a patriotic act. Driven by these two motivations, business activities became extremely individualistic in which the individual's short-term monetary gains were the overriding concern and the service element of the economic activities was completely ignored. This extreme individualism was responsible for the high incidence of consumer safety violations and environmental abuses in the early economic period, as well as business's casual attitude toward manufacturing counterfeit products. Today, Taiwan recognizes the hidden threats of individualistically oriented business behavior to its capitalist interests and concedes the urgent need for a community consciousness in all economic activities.

Deeply concerned by the potential social problems inherent in a society motivated by heated business competition, Kwoh-Ting Li, a major architect of Taiwan's economic development, has called for the adoption of a new moral principle that stresses obligation to community.[2] Laws designed to prohibit counterfeiting products and to protect the environment and consumers have now been established on the island. In addition, the number of corporations involved in establishing or funding educational institutions, and charity and welfare organizations is rising steadily. All these developments indicate that a community consciousness is in the making in Taiwan. Accordingly, we can expect environmental concerns, consumer interests, and other social issues to receive more attention from Taiwanese business and industry.

Economic growth requires steady changes in economic structure. In Taiwan, economic growth has been achieved by artificially introduced changes to the structure of its economy. In the past, planned growth orientations were focused, in sequence, on import substitution, export expansion, promotion of heavy and chemical industries, and high tech industry to guide and induce desired economic growth. As we think about the future course of Taiwan's economy, we wonder what kind of structural changes can be expected. In light of the large-scale appreciation of the currency and the overall relaxation of import controls that have recently taken place in Taiwan, we might find some clues. The appreciated currency has greatly strengthened the Taiwanese purchasing power in the international market, and the relaxation of Taiwan's import barriers has lifted the consumption constraints that were in place for decades in order to force savings. In addition, under U.S. pressure to open up its market to U.S. goods, the government has encouraged its citizens to spend.

The combined effect of these forces has been a massive increase in the country's consumption level. For example, as a result, Taiwan's entertainment industry including restaurants, travel, and recreation, have been enjoying a remarkable business boom. The unleashed demand for quality consumer products such as apparel, home furnishings, and automobiles, has brought the import businesses unprecedented prosperity. On the other hand, business and industry responded to their vastly increased power by investing heavily in manufacturing automation and product upgrade. These investments helped Taiwanese products to recover their competitiveness which they lost owing to the increased labor cost following the value adjustments from the appreciated local currency. The greatly appreciated Taiwanese currency led the resourceful to invest in international businesses and real estate. Such investments are expected to remove the latest inflation threat which originated in the sudden unleashing of purchasing power among consumers and industries.

In view of these changes, we may predict with some certainty that this trend of internally generated growth will continue into the near future, and the economy's export-originated growth will take on a new dimension owing to the country's vastly increased international investment activities. In addition, a more balanced economic structure in terms of consumption versus production and domestic market versus export market can be expected. With the decreased role of government in the economy, we will see more naturally evolving structural changes in the economy. Overall, we are witnessing Taiwan's transformation into a mature, market-function-driven, internationally relevant economy.

Taiwan's economy was built on its strong export performances. Through the years a certain distinct line of products has become the main force behind the nation's export strength, such as the agricultural products of the 1950s, the labor-intensive manufacturing products of the 1960s and 1970s, and the machine tools and electronic products of the 1980s. With the small size of the domestic market, the economy must depend on its export market for growth. The loss of competitiveness in labor cost to some other Southeast Asian countries has undermined the role of manufacturing as the supporting industry behind Taiwan's export strength. We may therefore ask, which industry is going to be Taiwan's next main export industry? In the past, the low-cost, high-quality assembly line workers helped build the country's light industry as its main export industry. Observers believe that Taiwan's rich human resources will continue dominant in shaping the major export industry. The rapid growth of Taiwan's computer and information industry and the strength of the engineering personnel resources suggest that this industry stands a good chance of becoming its major export industry.

When the Nationalist government took power in Taiwan, it had to contend with two political forces: the Communist threat from across the Formosa Straits, and the Taiwanese Independence Movement on the island. Interestingly, the island's economic success unexpectedly improved the Taiwanese standing with respect to both challenges. The half-century conflict between Nationalists and Communists in China was viewed by both sides as a contest of the superiority and suitability to China of the two ideologies—Communism and Dr. Sun Yat-Sen's Three Principles for the People—and of the better quality of life the regimes could offer their people. Taiwan's economic achievements, Communist China's recent concession of economic victory to its long-time political foe, and its public announcement of adopting the Taiwanese experience as its own model have given the Taiwanese government its long-awaited vindication. Communist China's decision to moderate its ideological hard line and to begin to experiment with capitalist principles has significantly relaxed tensions between the two Chinese regimes and may indeed have paved the way for their future reunification. The growth of Taiwan's economy requires better access to resources and material supplies as well as an expansion of its export market. Mainland China's rich endowment in natural resources and materials and its huge consumer market are the ideal answer to these needs. Taiwan is also eager to help modernize mainland China's economy. The collapse of communism in Eastern Europe and the recent reunification of the two Germanies have given the Taiwanese government yet more reasons to believe that the reunification of the two Chinas is inevitable. When it takes place, the Taiwanese, with their more advanced economy, will have a great deal to offer as well as to benefit from.

The Taiwanese Independence Movement grew out of the resentments which a small number of the island's old residents whose ancestors had immigrated from the mainland one to two hundred years ago, felt toward the newer immigrants. The movement calls for political separation between the old and new residents. Taiwan's economic success has brought particular prosperity to the old residents who, as a group, owned most of the land and capital. At the same time, the greatly improved quality of life on the island has given its people a more compromising spirit in dealing with social conflict. As a result, the movement has never been able to gather enough support to threaten internal stability. Material wealth has enhanced the people's enthusiasm in politics, and they demand progress in the political system. The democratization of the last two years has given birth to a true multiparty political system that has given the supporters of the movement a legitimate role in the country's politics. This process has produced long-desired social harmony. The relaxed confrontation between Nationalists and the Communists, the ensuing possibility of closer economic cooperation between mainland China and Taiwan, and the newly achieved social harmony may in fact have opened up a new chapter in Taiwan's political and economic life.

NOTES

1. See Simon Kuznets, "Modern Economic Growth and the Less Developed Countries," in Kwoh-Ting Li and Tzong-Shian Yu, eds., *Experiences and Lessons of Economic Development in Taiwan* (Taipei: Academia Sinica Press, 1982), pp. 11–20.

2. He called the new moral principle the Sixth Principle of Human Relations, meaning an addition to the five human relations Confucius had identified.

SELECTED BIBLIOGRAPHY

Andreski, Stanislav, ed. *Max Weber on Capitalism, Bureaucracy and Religion*. Boston: Allen & Unwin, 1983.

Barclay, George. *Colonial Development and Population in Taiwan*. Port Washington, N.Y.: Kennikat Press, 1972.

Bottomore, Tom. *Theory of Modern Capitalism*. Boston: Allen & Unwin, 1985.

Casson, Mark. *The Entrepreneur: An Economic Theory*. Totowa, N.J.: Barnes & Noble, 1982.

Cheng, Chu-Yuan. *Mainland China: Why Still Backward?* Taipei: Kuang Li, 1983.

Chesneaux, Jean, Francoise Le Barbier, and Marie-Claire Bergere. *China from the Nineteen Eleven Revolution to Liberation*. New York: Pantheon, 1977.

Chesneaux, Jean, Marianne Bastid, and Marie-Claire Bergere. *China from the Opium Wars to the Nineteen Hundred Eleven Revolution*. New York: Pantheon, 1976.

Cornwall, John. *Modern Capitalism: Its Growth and Transformation*. New York: St. Martin's Press, 1977.

Cowan, Charles. *The Economic Development of China and Japan*. New York: Praeger, 1964.

Deyo, Frederick, ed. *The Political Economy of the New Asian Industrialism*. Ithaca, N.Y.: Cornell University Press, 1987.

Doak, Barnett A. *China on the Eve of Communist Takeover*. New York: Praeger, 1963.

Dorn, Van, and Harold Archer. *Twenty Years of the Chinese Republic*. New York: Alfred A. Knopf, 1932.

Eastman, Lloyd. *The Abortive Revolution: China Under Nationalist Rule, 1927–1937*. Cambridge, Mass.: Harvard University Press, 1974.

Eisenstadt, Shmuel Noah, ed. *The Protestant Ethic and Modernization*. New York: Basic Books, 1968.

Fei, John. *Growth with Equality*. London: Oxford University Press, 1979.

Galenson, Walter. *Economic Growth and Structural Change in Taiwan: The Postwar Experience of the Republic of China.* Ithaca, N.Y.: Cornell University Press, 1979 .

———. *Foreign Trade and Investment.* Madison: University of Wisconsin Press, 1985.

Gentzler, J. Mason, ed. *Changing China: Readings in the History of China from the Opium War to the Present.* New York: Praeger, 1977.

Gold, Thomas. *State and Society in the Taiwan Miracle.* New York: Armonk, 1986.

Gray, Jack, ed. *Modern China's Search for a Political Form.* London: Royal Institute of International Affairs, Oxford University Press, 1969.

Green, Robert W. *Protestantism and Capitalism.* Boston: D.C. Heath, 1959.

Halal, William E. *The New Capitalism.* New York: Wiley, 1986.

Ho, Sam. *Economic Development of Taiwan 1860–1970.* New Haven, Conn.: Yale University Press, 1978.

Hornbeck, Stanley. *Contemporary Politics in the Far East.* New York: D. Appleton, 1916.

Hsing, Mo-Huan. *Taiwan: Industrialization and Policies.* London: Oxford University Press, 1971.

Jacob, Neil Herman. *U.S. Aid to Taiwan.* New York: Praeger, 1967.

Jacobs, Norman. *The Origin of Modern Capitalism and Eastern Asia.* London: Oxford University Press, 1958.

Jones, Leroy P., and I. L. Sakong. *Government, Business and Entrepreneurship in Economic Development: The Korean Case.* Cambridge, Mass.: Harvard University Press, 1980.

Kieffer, Martin. *The Awakening of China, 1793–1949.* New York: Putnam, 1967

Kilby, Peter, ed. *Entrepreneurship and Economic Development.* New York: Free Press, 1971.

Kin, W. Chan, and Philip Young, eds. *The Pacific Challenge in International Business.* Ann Arbor: University of Michigan Research Press, 1987.

Kuznets, Simon. *Economic Growth and Structure.* New York: Norton, 1965.

———. *Growth, Population, and Income Distribution.* New York: Norton, 1979.

———. *Modern Economic Growth—Rate, Structure, and Speed.* New Haven, Conn.: Yale University Press, 1966.

———. *Postwar Economic Growth.* Cambridge, Mass.: Belknap Press of Harvard University, 1964.

Li, Kwoh-Ting. *The Evolution of Policy Behind Taiwan's Development Success.* New Haven, Conn: Yale University Press, 1988.

Li, Kwoh-Ting, and Tzung-Shian Yu, eds. *Experience and Lessons of Economic Development in Taiwan,* Taipei: Academia Sinica Press, 1982.

Lin, Ching-Yuan. *Industrialization in Taiwan, 1946–1972.* New York: Praeger, 1973.

Lin, Sean-Ming. *A Study of the Development Process of New Industries in Developing Countries: A Case Study of the IC Industry in Taiwan.* Taiwan: National Taiwan University Press, 1987.

Lineborger, Paul. *The Political Doctrines of Sun Yat-Sen.* Baltimore: Johns Hopkins University Press, 1937.

Little, Ian M. D. *Economic Development, Theory, Policy, and International Relations.* New York: Basic Books, 1982.

Liu, Alan. *Phoenix and the Lame Lion: Modernization in Taiwan and Mainland China.* Stanford, Calif.: Stanford University Press, 1987.

Marshall, Gordon. *In Search of the Spirit of Capitalism.* New York: Columbia University Press, 1982.

Ohkawa, Kazushi, and Gustav Ranis, eds. *Japan and the Developing Countries.* New York: Oxford University Press, 1985.

Possi, Gianfranco. *Capitalism and the Capitalist Spirit.* Amherst, Mass.: University of Massachusetts Press, 1983.

Prybyla, Jan S. *The Societal Objectives of Wealth, Stability, and Equality in Taiwan.* Baltimore: University of Maryland Press, 1978.

Rabushka, Alvin. *The New China: Comparative Economic Development in Mainland China, Taiwan and Hong Kong.* Boulder: Westview Press, 1987.

Wang, Bio-Lu. *The Charm of a High Rate of Growth: The History of the Success of a Computer Giant.* Taipei: Time Publishing, 1988.

Wang, Tso-Yuong. *Economic Miracle.* Taipei: Time Publishing, 1984.

Weber, Max. *The Protestant Ethic and the Spirit of Capitalism.* Translated by Talcott Parsons. Boston: Allen & Unwin, 1956.

———. *The Religion of China.* Translated by Hans H. Gerth. Glencoe, Ill.: Free Press, 1951.

Wu, Yuan-Li. *Growth, Distribution, and Social Change.* Baltimore: University of Maryland Press, 1978.

Yu, Yin-Shih. *The Religious Ethics in China of the Last Centuries and Capitalism.* Taipei: Lienchien, 1987.

INDEX

ABOUT THE AUTHOR

Y. DOLLY HWANG is President of Northern Pacific International, a consulting firm. Dr. Hwang received a Ph.D. from the University of Minnesota.